THE BRIDGESTONE

DUBLIN FOOD GUIDE
2000-2001

JOHN McKENNA — SALLY McKENNA

ESTRAGON PRESS

FIRST PUBLISHED IN 2000

BY ESTRAGON PRESS

DURRUS

COUNTY CORK

© ESTRAGON PRESS

TEXT © JOHN & SALLY McKENNA

THE MORAL RIGHT OF THE

AUTHORS HAS BEEN ASSERTED

ISBN 1 874076 33 2

WRITTEN BY JOHN McKENNA

PUBLISHING EDITOR: SALLY McKENNA

ART DIRECTION: NICK CANN

EDITOR: JUDITH CASEY

PRINTED BY COLOUR BOOKS LTD

COVER PHOTOS
AYA Restaurant (Dublin) by Mark Nixon
All other photos by Mike O'Toole

■ All rights reserved. No part of this publication may be reproduced, stored in a retrieval system or transmitted in any form or by any means, without the prior permission of the publishers.

■ Whilst every effort has been made to ensure that the information given in this book is accurate, the publishers and authors do not accept responsibility for any errors or omissions or for any change in the circumstances of any of the entries.

FOR JEREMY ADDIS

WITH THANKS TO:

Des Collins

Colm Conyngham

Brian Condon

Nick Cann

Pat Young

Judith Casey

Yoichi Hoashi

Mike O'Toole

Ann Marie Tobin

Una Carmody

Paula Buckley

Frieda Forde

BRIDGESTONE

BRIDGESTONE is the world's largest tyre and rubber manufacturer.

■ Founded in Japan in 1931, it currently employs over 95,000 people in Europe, Asia and America and its products are sold in more than 150 countries. Its European plants are situated in France, Spain and Italy.

■ Bridgestone manufacture tyres for a wide variety of vehicles from passenger cars and motorcycles, trucks and buses to giant earthmovers and aircraft.

■ Many Japanese and European cars sold in Ireland have been fitted with Bridgestone tyres during manufacture and a host of exotic sports cars including Ferrari, Lamborghini, Porsche and Jaguar are fitted with Bridgestone performance tyres as original equipment.

■ Bridgestone commercial vehicle tyres enjoy a worldwide reputation for superior cost per kilometre performance and its aircraft tyres are used by more than 100 airlines.

■ In 1988 Bridgestone acquired the Firestone Tyre and Rubber Company combining the resources of both companies under one umbrella. This coupled with an intensive research and development programme has enabled Bridgestone to remain the world's most technologically advanced tyre company with testing centres in Japan, USA, Mexico and Italy.

■ Bridgestone tyres are distributed in Ireland by Bridgestone/Firestone Ireland Limited, a subsidiary of the multinational Bridgestone Corporation. A wide range of tyres are stocked in its central warehouse and staff provide sales, technical and delivery services all over Ireland.

■ Bridgestone tyres are available from tyre dealers throughout Ireland.

FOR FURTHER INFORMATION:

BRIDGESTONE/FIRESTONE IRELAND LTD
Unit 4
Leopardstown Office Park,
Dublin 18
Tel: (01) 295 2844
Fax: (01) 295 2858

34 Hillsborough Road,
Lisburn
BT28 1AQ
Tel: (01 846) 678331
Fax: (01 846) 673235

website: www.bridgestone-eu.com

BRIDGESTONE AWARDS

THE ICONS

The Bridgestone Icons are those cooks, shopkeepers and producers who offer the most outstanding food in the city.

CAVISTON'S DELICATESSEN
DUBLIN BREWING COMPANY
L'ECRIVAIN
THE GALLIC KITCHEN
HICK'S BUTCHERS
THE MERMAID CAFÉ
DANNY O'TOOLE BUTCHERS
SEARSON'S WINE MERCHANTS
SHERIDAN'S CHEESEMONGERS
THE TEMPLE BAR MARKET
THORNTON'S

THE CLASSICS

The Bridgestone Classics are those people who have contributed significantly to Dublin's culinary culture.

AYUMI-YA JAPANESE RESTAURANT
CHINA-SICHUAN
COOKE'S CAFÉ

BRIDGESTONE AWARDS

Dish
Downey's of Terenure
The Elephant & Castle
Fothergill's
Roy Fox
McCabe's Wine Merchants
The Morgan
Number 31
101 Talbot
The Tea Rooms
Terroirs

THE NEW WAVE

The Bridgestone New Wave are those cooks, shopkeepers and places to stay with the greatest potential to contribute to Dublin's culinary culture.

Aya
Ely
Epicurean Food Mall
Halo
La Maison des Gourmets
Nude
O'Connell's

The glorious world of Irish food and hospitality in three simple clicks...

bestofbridgestone.com

All about John and Sally McKenna's award-winning Bridgestone Guide series

bestofireland.org

Everything and everyone that's important in Irish food

johnmckenna.net

Recipes, food lore and a monthly newsletter from the food writer you simply have to read

INTRODUCTION

One can scarcely keep up to date with the frenetic pace of development in Dublin today, as the city powers ahead with new buildings and developments in every imaginable location. As it is with the city's economy, so it is with the city's food. You blink, and another couple of restaurants have opened. Take a breath, and a new shopping development has begun. Close your eyes for a second, and a clutch of new places to drink coffee, or a pair of new mega-pubs, have opened their doors. The city has never seen anything like it.

But, amidst all this mêlée, the great and the good of Dublin's food remain constant, and those are the people dealt with in greatest detail in this guide to the capital's food. The best shops, restaurateurs, markets, pubs and places to stay are all described in this book, which aims to provide the resident and the visitor with all the information they need to get the very best out of one of the world's great cities. If we cannot recommend a place, we have simply excluded it.

There has, truthfully, never been a better time to eat in Dublin. Both the quality of food and the choice of food has never been better or greater, and the booming economy has proven to be an enormous benefit to the finest places to eat and shop.

Just as importantly, Dublin retains its inimitable character despite the many changes visited on the city over the last decade and during the period that we have written books on the city's food culture. There is still nowhere like it, despite the traffic jams, and the litter problem and the other hassles of day to day living. There is still no other city where, at the close of the working day, one experiences an atmosphere which is both pacific and powerful, the calm before the raucous storm of evening time.

JOHN McKENNA, SALLY McKENNA

HOW TO USE THIS BOOK

THE BRIDGESTONE DUBLIN FOOD GUIDE describes the restaurants, shops and pubs of the city centre, and then organises other entries according to which of the outlying Dublin villages they are to be found in.

■ So Roly's Bistro, just south of the city centre, is found in the Southside chapter, under Ballsbridge, whilst The Old Schoolhouse, north of the city, is described, in the Northside chapter, under Swords.

■ Although these villages have been gradually subsumed under the cloak of a greater Dublin, they are still regarded by the residents as separate villages – independent republics, indeed – and all of them enjoy their own separate identity.

■ As the Temple Bar Market and the new Epicurean Food Hall both have their own separate identities, and are of significant importance, we have dealt with them separately.

■ Throughout the book, we have asked Dubliners to list some of their favourite and most essential addresses. These are of course personal choices, but you can trust that they are very well considered indeed.

CONTENTS

BRIDGESTONE TYRES 4

BRIDGESTONE AWARDS 6

INTRODUCTION 9

HOW TO USE THIS BOOK 10

CITY CENTRE 12

TEMPLE BAR MARKET 26

EPICUREAN FOOD MARKET 50

DUBLIN PUBS 62

SOUTHSIDE DUBLIN 66

COFFEE SHOPS & CAFES 74

NORTHSIDE DUBLIN 104

INDEX 124

CITY CENTRE

ASIA MARKET
Helen Pau
18 Drury Street, Dublin 2
Tel: (01) 677 9764

Helen Pau's shop is the most essential Asian store in the city, and contains everything your eastern cookery needs: if they haven't got it, chances are it doesn't exist. Brilliantly surreal music, helpful funky Irish staff, and of course that curiously cold and alienating lighting which is a feature of Chinese shops throughout the world.

- **OPEN:** 10am-7pm Mon-Fri, 11am-6pm Sat-Sun

AYA ❂
Yoichi Hoashi
Brown Thomas, Clarendon Street, Dublin 2
Tel: (01) 677 1544   mail@aya.ie   www.aya.ie

Ireland's first conveyor-belt sushi bar is to be found in AYA, located at the rere of the stylish Brown Thomas store, and this cool, hip spot has become one of the city's most irresistible eating houses in double-quick time.
The fun food-on-the-belt is only one part of AYA, which also offers a contemporary Japanese restaurant where Jennifer Glynn cooks, and a Japanese food hall with lots of freshly prepared cooked food-to-go as well as essential Japanese ingredients. Yoichi Hoashi and his team have always underpinned everything they do with good service, which is always joyously evident in Aya. Unmissable.

- **OPEN:** 7.30am-11pm Mon-Fri, 10am-11pm Sat, 11am-9.30pm Sun. Deli open 7.30am-7pm Mon-Fri, 10am-6pm Sat, noon-6pm Sun
- **AVERAGE PRICE:** Breakfast from £3, Lunch from £8, Dinner from £25

IL BACCARO
Diceman's Corner, Meeting House Square
Temple Bar, Dublin 2
Tel: (01) 671 4597

Il Baccaro is a little slice of Northern Italy transported with brilliant effect to Temple Bar. For hanging out late at night, with lots of cheap wine and some okay food and an atmosphere which cannot be found anywhere else in town, this

CITY CENTRE

little cave simply can't be beat. It's probably best to stick with the platters of cured meats and cheeses to soak up the agreeably cheap grog, for the more complex cooking isn't truly their strength. But, frankly, food is somewhat beside the point: the craic is where it's at, and at 2am, the person singing some forlorn Italian love song, accompanied by a strumming guitar, is most likely... well, you, actually.

- **OPEN:** 7pm-'till late
- **AVERAGE PRICE:** Meals £6-£15

BAD ASS CAFÉ
Brian Rowan
Temple Bar, Dublin 2
Tel: (01) 671 2596

A Temple Bar institution, the Bad Ass does what it has always done - pizzas, salads, wines - the way it has always done them. Kids enjoy all that pizza spinning and tossing, which means weary parents can chill out for a few minutes.

- **OPEN:** 11.30am-midnight Mon-Sun
- **AVERAGE PRICE:** Lunch £5, Dinner £10

BANG CAFÉ
The Stokes Brothers
11 Merrion Row, Dublin 2
Tel: (01) 676 0898
www.bangrestaurant.com

The Stokes brothers may not win any prizes for the food in their café, but their Dad should certainly get a gong for his design work in creating a superb series of rooms out of this awkward space: Bang is engagingly gorgeous, a clever trio of rooms (there is a lounge on top) which suit almost any time of the day.
The food can have its moments all right – butterleaf salad with blue cheese; calamari with remoulade which is well delivered; pork sausages with mash and apple sauce; lamb chops whose ratatouille for some reason has shiitake mushrooms in it. Service is pleasingly amateurish, though one suspects it might get a little stressed on busy nights. Somehow, though, the place works, but do take it with a light heart.

- **OPEN:** 10am-10.45pm (lunch 12.15pm-3pm, dinner from 6pm)
- **AVERAGE PRICE:** Lunch £15-£20, Dinner £30

CITY CENTRE

BANGKOK CAFÉ
Mo Hennessey
106 Parnell Street, Dublin 1
Tel: (01) 878 6618

Thank heavens for the pauvre style of the Bangkok, such a valuable antidote to the chrome and MDF of everywhere else in town. Mo Hennessey's Thai cooking is simple – mainly green and red curries, but all delivered with precision – the wine list has about four bottles on it which are stored in a Coke fridge, everything costs half nothing, service is great, and the place has the coolest cult audience you will find. Truly hip.

- **OPEN:** 5.30pm-10.30pm Mon-Sun
- **AVERAGE PRICE:** Dinner £12-£15

BELGO
John Dunne
Sycamore Street, Temple Bar, Dublin 2
Tel: (01) 672 7555

The moules-frites-beer chain Belgo has a big – 180 seater – series of rooms in Temple Bar, and has imported its beers and its Trappist monk uniforms to Dublin. The design is nifty, the clerical costumes of the waiting staff are hilariously camp, and the beers are terrific, but the moules-and-frites, waterzooi-and-other-Belgian-fare formula tastes like a formula, and prices are high for what you get.

- **OPEN:** Noon-3pm, 5pm-11pm Mon-Thur, noon-midnight Fri-Sat, noon-11pm Sun
- **AVERAGE PRICE:** Lunch from £5, Dinner £15

BERNARDOS
Loretta Gentile
19 Lincoln Place, Dublin 2
Tel: (01) 676 2471

Step in the door and you step back in time. Celebrated for their scampi and their ice creams, the food is perennial Irish-Italian, meaning it is neither one nor the other.

- **OPEN:** 12.30pm-2.30pm Mon-Fri, 6.15pm-11pm Mon-Sat
- **AVERAGE PRICE:** Lunch from £6, Dinner £16

CITY CENTRE

BERRY BROS & RUDD
Peter Foley
4 Harry Street, Dublin 2
Tel: (01) 677 3444

A most gorgeous wine shop, run with great skill and confidence by Peter Foley and his staff. The list is huge – about 1,300 wines all told – and the temperature-controlled cellars house many wallet-busting superstars, but Berry Bros' reputation has always been securely founded on their own well-made claret and a range of own-label wines, which are ever reliable and good value. It's a true pleasure to browse and shop in here.

- **OPEN:** 10am-7pm Mon-Sat (till 8pm Thur)

BEWLEY'S ORIENTAL CAFÉ
Trevor Brown
Grafton Street, Dublin 2
Tel: (01) 677 6761

The lovely room of Bewley's, with its Harry Clarke windows, remains a perennial delight, and taking coffee in here is one of the essential baptisms for any visitor to the city. The food is simple and obvious, but one just wishes that Bewley's would serve a good steak and salty hot fries and smooth creme caramel and jugs of rough wine, the sort of food that would perfectly suit a great brasserie room such as this.

- **OPEN:** 7am-11pm Mon-Sun
- **AVERAGE PRICE:** Meals£3-£20

THE BIG CHEESE Co.
David Brown & Sonia Bradford
Trinity Street, Dublin 2
Tel: (01) 671 1399

The Big Cheese is an excellent shop, whose fine range of artisan cheese from Ireland, England and Europe is matched by lots of smartly packaged foods, in particular American speciality foods. They also stock a range of kosher foods. A second branch has just opened in the Epicurean Mall on Liffey Street. Look out especially for their speciality breads.

- **OPEN:** 10am-6pm Mon-Sat

CITY CENTRE

BLAZING SALADS II
Lorraine Fitzmaurice
Powerscourt Townhouse, Dublin 2
Tel: (01) 671 9552

One of Dublin's culinary institutions, Blazing Salads is a venerable vegetarian restaurant, high up in the attic of the Powerscourt Townhouse. It offers consistent cooking, and thoughtfully provides certain dishes which are gluten, sugar, dairy and yeast-free for folk with allergy difficulties.

- **OPEN:** 10am-5.30pm Mon-Sat
- **AVERAGE PRICE:** Meals £5-£10

BOTTICELLI
Piro Cosso
3 Temple Bar, Dublin 2
Tel: (01) 672 7289

Botticelli gets closest to the virtues of simplicity and directness – and unpretentiousness – which we seek in Italian cooking. Its success can be explained by the fact that compromises are kept to a minimum – Italians would recognise what they do in here as something which they might find back home. Pastas, pizzas and coffee are all treated with respect, and mercifully there is no mucking about trying to put Irish inflections on Italian classics. Order some carpaccio, some pasta or gnocchi with mushrooms, skip dessert, have a ristretto and you get Botticelli at its best.

- **OPEN:** Noon-midnight Mon-Sun (from 1pm Sun)
- **AVERAGE PRICE:** meals £10

BROWNE'S BRASSERIE
Barry & Dee Canny
22 St Stephen's Green, Dublin 2
Tel: (01) 638 3939

This rather grand townhouse with rooms on St Stephen's Green houses a first-floor restaurant which borrows design styles from numerous sources and welds them together pretty effectively.
The food likewise mixes and matches – Caesar salad; squid with chilli oil; chicken and hazelnut terrine; confit of duck leg with fondant potatoes; fillet of brill with spaghetti of vegetables, creme brulée with marinated sultanas.

CITY CENTRE

The food may lack a distinct personality, but Browne's is fast getting a reputation as a good spot for meeting friends thanks to its location.

- **OPEN:** 12.30pm-3pm Mon-Fri, 6.30pm-10pm Mon-Sat
- **AVERAGE PRICE:** Lunch £20, Dinner £25

BRUNO'S
Bruno Berta
30 East Essex Street, Temple Bar,
Dublin 2
Tel: (01) 670 6767

21 Kildare Street, Dublin 2
Tel: (01) 6624724

The cooking in Bruno Berta's well-conceived room is ridiculously contemporary – strudel of chicken with mushroom lasagne; seared scallops with vanilla sabayon; mussels and Parma parmentier – but quibbling about the authenticity of Joe Forkan's cooking in Bruno's is the last thing on the minds of the folk who merrily eat and drink here. The regulars who pack the place love the fact that Bruno's is, in effect, the Trocadero of Temple Bar. The buzz is good, the service cocky, the energy raucous.
Bruno Berta has recently opened a second restaurant, in the basement of Mitchell's splendid wine shop on Kildare Street, and it has already got off to a good start as another atmospheric and enjoyable room.

- **OPEN:** Noon-11pm Mon-Sat
- **AVERAGE PRICE:** Lunch £11, Dinner £25

BU-ALI
Abi Abassali
28 Lower Clanbrassil Street, Dublin 8
Tel: (01) 454 6505

An authentic little Indian take-away with some tables where you can choose to eat. Its admirable plasticity and simplicity – a counter, some chairs, garish lighting, a bleating telly – are very echt. For the most part, it specialises as a take-away, and has a delivery service for the locality.

- **OPEN:** 5pm-2.30am Mon-Sat, 5pm-midnight Sun
- **AVERAGE PRICE:** Dinner from £8

SUPERMARKETS

The main supermarket players have all worked hard in recent years to both improve their stores, and to improve the variety of foods they offer right across the board.
In particular, they have all worked very hard on their respective wine shops and on developing the expertise of their wine shop staff, as they battle for market share with the wine specialists.

TESCO'S
flagship is at the Merrion Centre on Merrion Road, Dublin 4, (01-283 8274) and a recent redesign has substantially improved the supermarket. The Tesco store, Bloomfield's, in Dun Laoghaire, is particularly well-regarded by many folk.

SUPERQUINN'S
flagship is at the Blackrock Shopping Centre, south County Dublin (01-283 1511) and this affectionately regarded chain has stores dotted all around the city and the county. Staff are particularly helpful in the Superquinn stores, and do note that they have a very positive attitude towards maturing Irish farmhouse cheeses and selling them at their best condition.

DUNNES STORES'
flagship is at the St. Stephen's Green Shopping Centre, in the centre of the city (01-478 0188), and there are numerous branches dotted around the city, with another flagship store at Cornelscourt in south County Dublin.

ROCHES STORES'
flagship store is at the Frascati Shopping Centre, Blackrock, south County Dublin (01- 288 5391), and they have a useful city centre branch on Henry Street.

SUPERVALU
group, all of whose supermarkets are owned by individual owners, are dotted in suburban centres around the city. The group also operates the numerous Centra convenience stores.

Two much loved, smaller individual supermarkets are **Morton's** of Dunville Avenue in Ranelagh (see entry), and **Damien Kiernan's** excellent Supervalu on Mount Merrion, on the southside, (01- 288 1014), a supermarket prized by locals and by the many artisan producers who supply it.

CITY CENTRE

LEO BURDOCK'S
Charlie McGorchan
2 Werburgh Street, Dublin 8
Tel: (01) 454 0306

The original and best Dublin chipper has now spawned twin branches, one sited in Rathmines' Swan Centre (01- 497 3117), the second on the northside at 375 North Circular Road (01-830 4114).
Whilst Werburgh Street remains dedicated and devoted to the cause of fish and chips, the newer branches – gasp! – serve things like lasagne and chicken kiev!
The old timers, who have for decades queued in the rain at Werburgh Street to get their packet and their bottle of pop might be aghast, but let us remember that between the wars there were actually seven Burdock's fish and chip shops existing at one time, so the newer expansions are nothing new. And nothing new is what everyone likes about the original. Do make sure, when you finally arrive at the counter and order some whiting and chips, to ask for some crispy bits. That proves you are a true Dub.

- **OPEN:** 12.30pm-11pm Mon-Fri, 2pm-11pm Sat
- **AVERAGE PRICE:** Meals £4

CAFÉ AURIGA
Brian Rowan
Temple Bar Square, Dublin 2
Tel: (01) 671 8228

Auriga is a very stylish first floor room, with all the right sort of modern colours and furniture and typical Temple Bar fusion food: smashed potatoes; balsamic vegetables; chicken confit cooked in lemongrass on a potato rosti. The view across the square is only great.

- **OPEN:** 5.30pm-11pm Mon-Sat
- **AVERAGE PRICE:** Dinner £20

LA CAVE
Margaret Beskri
28 South Anne Street, Dublin 2
Tel: (01) 679 4409
www.lacavewinebar.com

The basement Cave is nostalgically decorated with bistro clichés in terms of posters and prints and red paper napkins,

and it serves agreeable and simple bistro dishes: goose rilettes; lamb with prunes; couscous aux sept legumes; tarte tatin; good coffee, and a great selection of wines.
Atmosphere is everything, and Margaret Beskri and her glamorous team handle the late night crew with just the right touch – everyone loves La Cave, one of the cult Dublin addresses.

- **OPEN:** 12.30pm-2am Mon-Sat, 6pm-2am Sun
- **AVERAGE PRICE:** Lunch £7, Dinner £16

THE CEDAR TREE
Ismail Sarhan
11 St. Andrew's Street,
Dublin 2
Tel: (01) 677 2121

The cooking offers various Lebanese specialities in this low-key, left-field, long-lived basement restaurant where a lot of folk like to hang out late at night to drink wine and eat mezzes.

- **OPEN:** 5.30pm-11pm Mon-Sun
- **AVERAGE PRICE:** Dinner £22

THE CHAMELEON
Carol Walshe & Vincent Vis
1 Fownes Street Lower, Temple Bar,
Dublin 2
Tel: (01) 671 0362

Magisterially masterminded by the vivacious bonhomie of Carol Walshe, and with Vincent Vis in firm control of the cooking, Chameleon is Temple Bar's Mom'n'Pop place, a shrine devoted to the caring work of these two people.
Walk in the door and you get character and charm thanks to the style and the service. Sit down and you get a sassy style of Indonesian cooking which Mr Vis understands perfectly: Nasi Goreng, fried rice with various meats, strips of omelette and krupuk crackers – Satays served with katjan sauce and gado gado – Bami Goreng, noodles with beansprouts, ginger and garlic with a choice of meats.

- **OPEN:** 6pm-11pm Tue-Sat (Sun closed 10pm)
- **AVERAGE PRICE:** Dinner £13.50-£21.50

DUBLINER'S CHOICE

JILLIAN BOLGER'S FIVE ESSENTIAL ADDRESSES

1

THE MERMAID CAFÉ
Sexy food, sexy staff, sexy surroundings.

2

MULLIGANS ON POOLBEG STREET
A taste of old Dublin - and a damn fine hot whiskey too.

3

THE BANGKOK CAFE
Affordable, authentic, memorable Thai food - so good you won't mind the decor.

4

JUSTIN & MARINA
in George's Street Arcade (currently changing its name since new owners took it over in Dec). Produce is presented in an appealing, friendly manner - everything is labelled clearly so as not to intimidate - these people want to educate and convert us, and with such passion.

5

CAFÉ MAO
Busy, buzzy place with deliciously healthy food. I could eat here 5 days a week (and have often tried to!).

Jillian Bolger is editor of Food & Wine Magazine

CITY CENTRE

CHAPTER ONE
Ross Lewis
18/19 Parnell Square, Dublin1
Tel: (01) 873 2266

Ross Lewis has a keen business clientele for his well-realised food: bavarois of red peppers with tapenade & aubergine discs; boudin of chicken foie gras with creamed leeks and mustard; superb roast brill with a crust of potatoes and cep sauce which is exactingly delivered; delicate saffron poached pear with pinenut and raisin parfait and orange caramel. The room is comfortable, service is confident, and Chapter One is a key address in this culinarily-deprived part of town.

- **OPEN:** 12.30pm-2.30pm, 6pm-10.30pm Tue-Fri, 6pm-10.30pm Sat
- **AVERAGE PRICE:** Lunch £16, Dinner from £16

CHILI CLUB
Sharon Kenna
Anne's Lane, Sth Anne Street
Dublin 2
Tel: (01) 677 3721

The Chili Club preceded the current boom in all things Thai and Asian, and its popularity endures because its satays are crisply tactile and its curries are sweetly milky and gently spicy, and desserts are good. It's very easy to enjoy this food, and this intimate little room has plenty of character.

- **OPEN:** 12.30pm-2.30pm Mon-Sat, 6pm-11pm Mon-Sun (till 11.30pm Thu-Sat)
- **AVERAGE PRICE:** Lunch £10, Dinner £20

THE COMMONS RESTAURANT
Michael Fitzgerald
Newman House, St Stephen's Green, Dublin 2
Tel: (01) 475 2597

The Commons Restaurant occupies the basement of the beautiful Newman House, and offers modern French cooking with some interesting twists, served in the true bourgeois fashion with meticulous attention. There is a verandah at the rere which is very enjoyable on a sunny summer lunchtime.

- **OPEN:** 12.30pm-2.15pm Mon-Fri, 7pm-10.15pm Mon-Sat
- **AVERAGE PRICE:** Lunch £20, Dinner £35

CITY CENTRE

COOKE'S CAFÉ & THE RHINO ROOM ©
John Cooke
14 Sth William Street, Dublin 2
Tel: (01) 679 0536/7/8 Rhino Room: (01) 670 5260

John Cooke is one of the most intelligent chefs in Dublin, and has successfully steered his way through the food fashions of the last decade with skill, mainly by concentrating on the sort of food which we might call modern classical: black bean soup; Caesar salad, aged sirloin of beef (all of these done to perfection, it should be said), scallops with angel hair pasta; veal kidney with celeriac. For some people, the subtlety of Cooke's is just too subtle, but that subtlety is truly the soul of this restaurant. The upstairs Rhino Room is a calmer space, the food just as polished and intelligent.

- **OPEN:** Café: 12.30pm-3pm, 6pm-11pm Mon-Sun (Sun closed 10pm). Rhino Room: 10.30am-11.30pm Tue-Sat
- **AVERAGE PRICE:** Café lunch from £14.50, Dinner from £30; Rhino Room lunch £9.95, Dinner £20-£25

CORNUCOPIA
Deirdre McCafferty
19 Wicklow Street, Dublin 2 Tel: (01) 677 7583

Eddie Bates has transformed the cooking in Cornucopia, which remains Dublin's favourite vegetarian restaurant. Mr Bates has lightened the rather traditional style of food, though the lunchtime formula of staples and salads endures, probably because so many people like it. The room is nicely informal, a mix of tables and counters along the window, with table service at weekend nights when Bates has a greater chance to show his talents.

- **OPEN:** 9am-8pm Mon-Sat, 9am-9pm Thu
- **AVERAGE PRICE:** meals around £6

DA PINO
Iris and Sarah
38/40 Parliament Street, Temple Bar
Tel: (01) 671 9308

Along with the Elephant & Castle, this is the closest Temple Bar gets to a neighbourhood restaurant.
Familiar, friendly and fun, which is just what you would say of the likable pasta 'n' pizza style of food they serve.

- **OPEN:** Noon-midnight
- **AVERAGE PRICE:** Meals from £5

CITY CENTRE

DAIL BIA
Sinéad Ní Fhlanagáin
46 Kildare Street
Dublin 2
Tel: (01) 670 6079

Dail Bia is a venture which was begun by the co-ordinating body of voluntary Irish language organisations in the country and further backed by the department of the Arts, Heritage, Gaeltacht and Islands, the sort of origin which might make it sound very schoolmarmy and well-meaning. But Sinéad Ní Fhlanagáin's sleek basement room with its stone walls and ash floor is stylish and the cooking, whilst simple, is good daytime food prepared with care.

- **OPEN:** 7.30am-6pm Mon-Fri, 9.30am-5pm Sat

DIEP LE SHAKER
Matthew Farrell
55 Pembroke Lane,
Dublin 2
Tel: (01) 661 1829

A stylish room on two levels and a sassy crowd got the Shaker off to a quick start, and its polyglot Asian food — it offers both Chinese and Thai dishes — has proven popular, though purists may question the authenticity of two such diverse cuisines being offered side-by-side. The smart city crowd who turn up here are more concerned about having a good time, however, than to be worrying about what is or is not truly echt.

- **OPEN:** 12.20pm-2.15pm Mon-Fri, 6.30pm-10.30pm Mon-Wed, 6.30pm-11.15pm Thur-Sat.
- **AVERAGE PRICE:** Lunch £15-£20, Dinner over £20

DISH ©
Trevor Browne & Gerard Foote
2 Crow Street, Temple Bar
Dublin 2
Tel: (01) 671 1248

There are many too many opportunists running restaurants in Temple Bar and too few true restaurateurs, but Dish — and a handful of others — is proof that the skills of the true professionals will win out. Trevor Browne and Gerard Foote's restaurant makes the maximum use of an awkward space, and the youthful verve – and the superlative music – which animate this room are a thrill. Whilst the cooking is modern, it is not the slightest bit gratuitous, and it succeeds because it is both well understood and well accomplished: organic beef carpaccio with roasted aubergine; smoked chicken hash with basted eggs; blackened chicken Caesar salad; hake with peppered spinach. Dish is terrific for Sunday brunch, when the cool sounds create the perfect atmosphere. A key address.

- **OPEN:** 11.30pm-11.30pm Mon-Sun
- **AVERAGE PRICE:** Lunch from £10, Dinner from £20

DOBBINS WINE BAR
John O'Byrne
15 Stephen's Lane
Dublin 2
Tel: (01) 676 4679

This legendary restaurant breaks all the rules. It's based in a Nissen hut down a little lane, yet it pulls in a million and a half quid a year. It is populated by the fashionable and powerful, yet it has sawdust on the floor and gingham table cloths, and Gary Flynn's food is far from the cutting edge. But when you eat in Dobbins, you know why it has endured for 21 years. Service is superb, the atmosphere is acute, and the food is enjoyable. Above all, John O'Byrne runs a supremely sociable restaurant, the sort of place from where you call the office at 4pm to tell them you won't be back.

- **OPEN:** 12.30pm-3pm Mon-Fri, 7.30pm-11.30pm Tue-Sat
- **AVERAGE PRICE:** Lunch £16, Dinner £25

DRUID CHOCOLATES
Gareth Vaughan
St. Paul's North King Street
Dublin 7
Tel: (01) 677 1026

This small company makes an attractive range of fresh cream chocolates, sold in better delicatessens around the town. Enjoy them one at a time, when their impact is greatest.

- **OPEN:** Sold locally in delis

TEMPLE BAR MARKET

From Mexico to Italy, from sushi to sausages, from organics to olives and crepes to chickens, the Saturday Temple Bar Market is the best thing to have happened to the city in years. The talented people who turn up here each Saturday and set up their stalls have created a fabulous artisan market, something the city had been crying out for for decades. The following are some of the major marketeers, but they are consistently supplemented by others who sell whatever produce is available at different times of the year.

BREAD BIN
Home made bread from Karen and Paul Coleman.

CHEZ EMILY
Helena Hemeryck makes exceedingly fine chocolates, acclaimed by a tasting test held by a group of young women in The Irish Times as "the best chocolates we had ever tasted – each one tasted amazingly good, and different, and not too sweet".

CORLEGGY CHEESE
Silke Cropp drives down from Belturbet in County Cavan each Saturday to sell her splendid Corleggy and Drumlin cheese. Look out for the smoked Drumlin cheeses, smoked by Frank Hederman, and for the fresh cheese and the baby Corleggys, which can only be bought here.

CRUMBLES & CO
Look out for the Thyme to Eat foods made by Suzanne Nolan.

DRUMEEL FARM
Pat Cremin comes down from County Longford each weekend to sell excellent venison – so young it doesn't even need to be marinaded – and he also sells free-range chickens, lamb and good eggs. "I know what happens to the food from conception to consumer," says Pat.

DUNNE & CRESCENZI
See page 29 for details of this wonderful specialist Italian food & wine importers. In the Temple Bar market they concentrate on cheeses brought directly from Italy.

THE GALLIC KITCHEN
The city's great baker keeps getting better and better, and if you need proof, just buy one of Sarah Webb's finnan haddie quiches, ask them to warm it through for you, then sit in

Meetinghouse Square as the market unfolds and dissolve into sheer bliss as you eat this masterpiece, made using Frank Hederman's smoked haddock. Perfection! But then so is everything else Ms Webb bakes, from the pinto bean burritos to the potato cakes (for Sunday breakfast), the soups, the basil and mozzarella tarts, the splendid sweet baking.

GOING BANANAS
Juices from Richard Brennan.

GLENCARN FOODS
Hugh Robson's stall offers the most brilliant organic meats from his farm in The Burren in County Clare. The sausages and bacon are only mighty, the lamb and chickens terrific, and the black and white puddings, made by Sarah Robson, are as fine as you will find. You will find some of the foods – cooked - in Ely, a lovely restaurant and wine bar in the city run by Hugh's son, Erik.

HEALYS VEGETABLES & FRUIT
Denis and Hilary Healy sell organic fruit and vegetables from their stall, with rarities such as wild frauchans ((it takes an hour to pick one jar!) alongside tiny baby cauliflowers, Sharps Express spuds, laundry-white bak choi, baby cucumbers, and tiny salad potatoes known as "Denis and Hilary's babies".

HICKS BUTCHERS
The peerless pork butcher of the southside has been one of the market stalwarts, his brilliant bangers and outstanding kassler some of the best foods made in Ireland. The variety of sausages is terrific – cajun sausages, orange and fennel; bratwurst; chorizo; wine and garlic; Moroccan merguez – and do buy a cooked banger from the barbecue.

THE JAPANESE FOOD CO
Sushi, sold under the label Sue's Sushi, made by Maggy in Dublin 7.

THE KOREAN FOOD CO
Paul McGrath offers a taste of the east.

McNALLY FAMILY FARM
Farm produce from Jenny McNally's farm in Naul.

OLVI OILS
Miriam Griffith's little food company has been one of the most delightful successes in recent years, with her range of flavoured oils and olive preserves slowly expanding and developing in a logical, organic way. Do ask for her tips on using them in sandwiches.

THE BRIDGESTONE DUBLIN FOOD GUIDE

TEMPLE BAR MARKET

THE PURE VEG
Richard Crooke sells vegetables from his farm in Bray.

ANNE ROSSITER FOODS
Anne sells a lovely mix of sweet and savoury baking – carrot cake; polenta, lemon and almond cake; baklava; broccoli quiche; spanokopitta – all with a handmade touch.

SABORES DE MEXICO
"We make the foods the way they make them in Mexico," say Gus and Theresa Hernandez, and if you want authenticity in your Mexican cooking – and you do – then you need to know about their corn tortillas, refried beans; jalapenos in escabeche, and their flamy chilli sauces and achiote paste, foods with the real flavours of Mexico.

ST. MARTIN SHELLFISH
Half a dozen native oysters fresh from the west coast should get the weekend off to a good start, and the McInerney family stall is where you will find these scintillating County Clare shellfish.

SHERIDAN'S CHEESEMONGERS
The superstars of cheese selling are market men at heart. Seamus and Kevin Sheridan kicked off their business in the Galway market (where they still sell on Saturdays) before expanding eastwards to the city. Their knowledge of cheese – who makes it, how they make it, when it is ready – is unsurpassed, and everything they sell is good, the cheeses from the Continent as well looked after as the Irish farmhouse cheeses.

SWEDISH BUNS
A stall run by Carla Medina MacNamara now of Lucan.

THE REAL OLIVE CO.
Of course, you cannot have a market in Ireland unless Toby Simmonds' Real Olive Stall is involved, and not just involved but right at the heart and soul of the action. You will have to join a maul of a queue to buy what you want, but it's worth the wait: great olives, great oils, great specialities such as wild garlic pesto and marinated garlic.

THE WABBIT CO.
"I'm a real cottage industry," says Brighid Goulet-Diskin, "because I work in a cottage!" Brighid's fudge is the real thing – "A lot of things sold as fudge are not fudge: it must be buttery but also crumbly." That's what the Wabbit Co.'s fudges are like.

● **OPEN:** The market is open 9am-5pm on Saturday

CITY CENTRE

THE DUBLIN FOOD CO-OP
Gerry Boland
St Andrew's Centre, Pearse Street, Dublin 2
Tel: (01) 873 0451

"The Co-Op is not simply a shop," says Gerry Boland of the managing committee of the Co-Op. "It is a trading entity concerned with food production, fair trade and the environment." Indeed it is, and has been for seventeen years now, with a core of volunteers and growers and stall holders making it someplace special to head to every Saturday morning. Almost everything sold here is organic or biodynamically produced, and even amongst the dried goods the percentage of organic foods is about 90%. But it's not just a visionary organisation: the vegetables produced by growers such as Penny Lange and Laura Turner are as fine as you will find in the country, and don't miss the organic milk, the Inisglass breads, the Sage baking, and the many other treats.

● **OPEN:** 9.30am-3pm Sat

DUNNE & CRESCENZI
Eileen & Stefano Crescenzi
14 South Frederick Street
Tel: (01) 677 3815   crescenz@esatclear.ie

The Crescenzis' Italian artisan foods are exceptionally good, and hugely superior to the branded labels available in other shops and supermarkets. Look out for the superb risotto rice, polenta, and pulses, as well as the artisan pastas and preserves. Their wine range is also singular and impressive, and it is a special treat to enjoy a glass of wine and a canape in the shop as you select all the things you just must take home with you.

● **OPEN:** 10.30am-7pm Mon-Sat

L'ECRIVAIN
Derry & Sally Anne Clarke
112 Lower Baggot St, Dublin 2
Tel: (01) 661 1919

Derry Clarke is the champion cook of the city. His progress towards his smart new 80-seater restaurant has been steady rather than spectacular, but the wisdom and sophistication and maturity of his cooking today cannot be

CITY CENTRE

matched in Dublin. He will serve Castletownbere scallops with a roasted shellfish sauce and a little filo parcel of the corals from the scallops, and the sheer perfection of the dish takes your breath away, so profound is his understanding of the flavours and his ability to exactly achieve what he wants. His buttermilk and lime sorbet is magnificent, his cappuccino soup of pumpkin and lemongrass sublime; his classic dishes such as baked rock oysters with cured bacon and cabbage and a Guinness sabayon, or deep fried Dublin Bay prawns with ketaifi pastry, tartare sauce and chilli jam, amongst the great Dublin dishes of our time.

Service, led by Sally-Anne Clarke, is perfect, the room is quite lovely, and value for money is exceptional.

- **OPEN:** 12.30pm-2pm Mon-Fri, 7pm-11pm Mon-Sat (early bird 6.30pm Mon-Thur £17.50)
- **AVERAGE PRICE:** Lunch £13.50-£16.50, Dinner from £25-£31.50

EDEN
Jay Bourke & Eoin Foyle
Meeting House Square
Temple Bar,
Dublin 2
Tel: (01) 670 5372

Eleanor Walsh's intuitive, sophisticated and earthy cooking in the lovely Eden has always had many champions, though the same can hardly be said for a restaurant about which people hold strong opinions regarding the style and the service – either you think the design is great and the staff fun and funky, or else you hate the place and want to sack all the staff straightaway because of their attitude.

But the food is smart, and shows a lot of the simple wisdom and respect for ingredients that Ms Walsh learnt while working in Cooke's Café: duck liver crostini; deep-fried halloumi cheese with aubergine salad; bacon and savoy cabbage risotto; lamb's liver with champ; terrific organic sirloin of beef with chips and bearnaise; rhubarb creme brulée.

The gutsy dishes tend to be the best, and they can show an elementalism which is beyond criticism. On a summer lunchtime, the verandah on Meeting House Square is special, and do try to get an outside table when they screen classic movies in the square on a summer's evening.

- **OPEN:** 12.30pm-3pm, 6pm-10pm Mon-Sun
- **AVERAGE PRICE:** Lunch £13-£15, Dinner £20

CITY CENTRE

ELEPHANT & CASTLE ●
Liz Mee & John Hayes
18 Temple Bar, Dublin 2
Tel: (01) 679 3121

We have a friend who has been known, when driving from Derry home to Dun Laoghaire, to detour into town, into the traffic jams, just to have the spicy chicken wings in the E&C. He is not alone: there are many people addicted to one or other of the classic dishes which they cook here, and which they cook better than anyone else.

Liz Mee and John Hayes created the most successful restaurant of the last decade, opening up in Temple Bar when no one else wanted to, and managing what everyone else believed was impossible: to serve good food through the entire day at good prices. They did it, and they have been doing it for more than ten years now and the reason why they continue to do it is simple: they are endlessly self-critical people, and they care about their customers.

The daily specials are chalked on the blackboard and many regulars opt for these, but others, who have been eating here for a decade, never get far beyond the chicken wings and the omelettes and the burgers and the ice cream and the yogurt frou-frou. Folk with young kids should note that the E&C is simply terrific for Sunday brunch.

- **OPEN:** 8am-11.30pm Mon-Fri, 10.30am-11.30pm Sat, noon-11pm Sun
- **AVERAGE PRICE:** Lunch £4-£14, Dinner £15-£20

ELY ●
Erik Robson
22 Ely Place, Dublin 2
Tel: (01) 676 8986

Watch out! The Robson dynasty is extending its tasteful food tentacles throughout the city. You can buy Dad Robson's superlative organic meats at the Temple Bar market (that is if the other stall holders haven't snapped them up before anyone else has a chance), sister Sarah has started a small company making excellent salad dressings, and now son Erik has brought together his wine expertise and his instinctive good taste to create Ely, one of the best new addresses in the city. The food can be superb: Robson's sausages and mash are benchmark, and the Irish stew, made with their organic lamb, is masterly. In addition, there are dozens of terrific wines, many of them available by the glass.

CITY CENTRE

Great sounds, great service, good coffee, and all told Ely is a mightily impressive new place.
By the by, could we suggest that they serve a true Dublin coddle, made with their good bacon and bangers and spuds? The city needs someone to resurrect the status of its only original dish, and no one else is doing it as well and as carefully as it should be done, and no one could do it as well as Erik Robson's Ely. We wait in hope.
Note: No reservations taken.

- **OPEN:** Noon-3pm, 5.30pm-10pm (last drink order at midnight)
- **AVERAGE PRICE:** Meals £2.95-£12.95

FINDLATER (WINE MERCHANTS)
Alex Findlater
The Harcourt Street Vaults,
10 Upper Hatch Street, Dublin 2
Tel: (01) 475 1699

We find the style of the Findlater's cellars to be rather old-fashioned and rather gloomy, not the most conducive atmosphere in which to buy wines. But their list is impressive, and boasts many of the great marques of the wine world – Baron Philippe de Rothschild, Penfolds, Veuve Cliquot, Concha Y Toro and many others.

- **OPEN:** 9am-6pm Mon-Fri, 10.30am-6pm Sat

LES FRERES JACQUES
Jean-Jacques Callibet
74 Dame Street, Dublin 2
Tel: (01) 679 4555

At a time when food fashions have become ridiculous in Dublin, with restaurants offering a grab-bag of cuisines instead of real, thoughtful cooking and properly composed menus, thank heavens for the mellow style of French classical cooking which prevails in Les Freres Jacques. Peasant soup; snails in garlic butter; sole on the bone; grilled lobster; roast lamb; creme caramel.
This is ageless food in an ageless place which is popular with an older generation, and one's only cavil is that, away from the set menus, prices can add up very quickly.

- **OPEN:** 12.30pm-2.30pm Mon-Fri, 7.30pm-10.30pm Mon-Sat
- **AVERAGE PRICE:** Lunch £15, Dinner £22

CITY CENTRE

THE GALLIC KITCHEN
Sarah Webb
49 Francis Street, Dublin 8
Tel: (01) 454 4912

This is the shop and café of the best baker in the city – see the entry for The Gallic Kitchen in the Temple Bar Market.

- **OPEN:** 9am-5pm Mon-Sat

GOOD WORLD RESTAURANT
Thomas Choi
18 Sth Great George's Street, Dublin 2
Tel: (01) 677 5373

The Good World does superb Dim Sum, and is popular with the Chinese community precisely for this reason. Their expertise with these little dishes is something to relish, cooking with dazzling verve and complexity: the kow-choi used to stuff some vegetable dumplings; the green peas used to top out some coriander dumplings; the curry powder used to electrify the wonderful fried pork skin and fish balls; the dazzling cheung fun; the lovely crisp fun-quor. Go early on Sunday mornings to make sure that you get a table upstairs: downstairs has zilch atmosphere.

- **OPEN:** 12.30pm-3am Mon-Sun
- **AVERAGE PRICE:** Lunch £7.50, Dinner £16

THE GOTHAM CAFÉ
David Barry
5 South Anne Street, Dublin 2
Tel: (01) 679 5266

This is a fun place, decorated with old Rolling Stone covers on the walls, packed with youngsters trying desperately to appear cool. Its fame rests with its pizzas, which are regarded by many folk as the best pizzas in the city, understandable when you consider the Gotham is related to the celebrated Independent Pizza Co of Drumcondra. Like the pizzas, the food is very Cal-Ital: goat's cheese crostini; chargrilled chicken with peanut sauce; penne with chilli and creole sausage; warm spicy prawn salad.

- **OPEN:** Noon-midnight Mon-Sat, noon-10.30pm Sun
- **AVERAGE PRICE:** Meals £7

CITY CENTRE

GUY STUART
Jenny Guy & Laragh Stuart
George's Street Arcade, Dublin 2
Tel: (01) 617 4827

Jenny Guy and Laragh Stuart are smart operators who run a very busy food-to-go operation with imaginative and delicious food. Soups and sandwiches are exceptionally good and there are good relishes and dips as well. Guy Stuart produce is available both wholesale and retail from the Arcade, and you will actually find their food served in many city delis.

- **OPEN:** 10.30am-6pm Mon-Sat (wholesale telephone orders taken from 8.30am)

RESTAURANT PATRICK GUILBAUD
Patrick Guilbaud
21 Upper Merrion Street, Dublin 2
Tel: (01) 676 4192

Patrick Guilbaud's restaurant does things in the classic, traditional French style, and has been rewarded by those guidebooks who admire that style with the requisite stars and rosettes and whatnot. Our opinion differs considerably, a stance which has caused considerable controversy and which has been interpreted by some as a publicity stunt on behalf of the Bridgestone guides. It's not a stunt. We admire the smooth professionalism of RPG as much as anyone, but the high prices and grand reputation should be matched by creative, exciting cooking, and that is absent here.

- **OPEN:** 12.30pm-2pm, 7.30pm-10.15pm Tue-Sat
- **AVERAGE PRICE:** Lunch and Dinner over £30

THE HARBOURMASTER
Sharon Hollywood
Custom House Dock, IFSC
Tel: (01) 670 1668

This large pub-cum-restaurant has been a hit right from the start, and its success can be gauged by the number of folk who find themselves eating here again and again.

- **OPEN:** Noon-3pm, 5pm-10.30pm Mon-Sat, 5pm-10.30pm Sun. Bar food served noon-8pm
- **AVERAGE PRICE:** Meals over £15

CITY CENTRE

HALO ☯
Jean-Michel Poulot
Morrison Hotel, Ormond Quay, Dublin 1
Tel: (01) 878 2999

The most fashionable room in town has been joined by LOBO, a new sushi bar, which complements the elegant fusion cooking of Halo. Jean Michel Poulot's supremely confident fusion food can produce hugely exciting flavours, though occasionally service fails to match the slick cooking.

- **OPEN:** 12.30pm-2pm, 7pm-10.30pm Mon-Sun
- **AVERAGE PRICE:** Lunch £20, Dinner £40

IMPERIAL CHINESE RESTAURANT
Mrs Cheung
12a Wicklow Street, Dublin 2
Tel: (01) 677 2580

The cooking in The Imperial tends towards the familiar notes of Sichuanese cooking adapted for Western tastes - steamed sea bass with ginger; beef and black bean sauce - so to see it at its best, go on a Sunday lunchtime, for their sublime dim sum. Glutinous rice in lotus leaf; prawns in rice paper; shark's fin dumpling; spicy chicken feet; squid and pork crackling, delicate and complex cookery achieved with finesse. Prices are tremendously keen.

- **OPEN:** Noon-midnight (dim sum 12.30pm-5.30pm) Mon-Sun
- **AVERAGE PRICE:** Lunch £10, Dinner £20

JACOB'S LADDER
Adrian & Bernie Roche
4-5 Nassau Street, Dublin 2
Tel: (01) 670 3865

Adrian and Bernie Roche have created one of the most exciting and enjoyable of the new Dublin restaurants, miraculously turning an unprepossessing series of rooms into the elegant style of Jacob's Ladder. The style impresses because of its leanness and lack of clutter, a factor which is the most significant characteristic of Roche's cooking. His extraordinary shellfish coddle – the Dublin dish of the last decade – was designed not merely to renovate the original, but to be much lighter on the palate, and he brings this intention to everything: superlative scallops with beetroot; home-smoked sea

CITY CENTRE

trout with marinated potatoes; salmon with carrageen and tomato broth; warm chocolate fondant. The rooms enjoy smashing views out over the playing fields of Trinity, and this is one of the cult addresses of the city.

- **OPEN:** 12.30pm-2.30pm, 6pm-10.30pm Tue-Sat
- **AVERAGE PRICE:** Lunch £15, Dinner £26

THE JOOSE BAR
Melanie Mercer & Emer Fitzpatrick
7a Poolbeg Street, Dublin 2

Melanie and Emer switched careers to open up the likable Joose, where they concentrate on vividly flavoured, healthful juices such as The Hair of the Dog (pink grapefruit, lemon, lime and orange juice – shift that hangover!) along with wraps, salads and sandwiches made with ciabatta. 7am opening means there's time to clear up those red eyes before you hit the office.

- **OPEN:** From 7am Mon-Sat

JUICE
David Keane
73 Sth Great George's Street, Dublin 2
Tel: (01) 475 7856

Juice is a very cool place, indeed almost self-consciously so, and at the weekend it stays open until 4am, when it will be filled with self-consciously cool night owls all drinking juices in order to shake off the booze of the evening. This is when it is at its best – during the day the food is a polyglot style of modern vegetarian cooking which can have some good moments, but service can be wayward.

- **OPEN:** Noon-11pm Sun, 9am-11pm, Mon-Wed, 9am-4am Thu-Fri, noon-4am Sat
- **AVERAGE PRICE:** Lunch from £4-£6, £15-£20

KHYBER TANDOORI
Shoaib Yunus
44/45 South William Street, Dublin 2
Tel: (01) 670 4855

Sam Hussain's restaurant prides itself on the authenticity of its Pakistani cooking, though the extensive menu also offers lots of dishes traditionally associated with familiar eastern

CITY CENTRE

cooking found in other ethnic restaurants in the city. Curiously enough, you are met at the door by a chap in traditional costume.

- **OPEN:** Noon-2.30pm, 6pm-midnight Mon-Sat, 5.30pm-11.30pm Sun
- **AVERAGE PRICE:** Lunch £7.50, Dinner £25

KILKENNY DESIGN
Catherine Curran
6 Nassau Street
Dublin 2
Tel: (01) 677 7066

The Kilkenny shop is a vital source of desirable home implements and objects from some of Ireland's best designers, but don't overlook the cooking in the upstairs café, where one counter serves substantial self-service lunches, whilst another dispenses speedy sandwiches. It's a good spot for coffee, and for peering out at the playing fields of Trinity, and various preserves and condiments are for sale, attractively packaged, which makes them desirable to give as presents.

- **OPEN:** 9am-9pm Mon-Sat (till 8pm Thur)
- **AVERAGE PRICE:** Meals under £10

KITCHEN COMPLEMENTS
Ann McNamee
Chatham Street
Dublin 2
Tel: (01) 677 0734

This is the best kitchen shop in town, with a veritable roll-call of all the great cooking names for sale alongside every manner of new kitchen implement, gee-gaw and necessity. Ann McNamee is a tireless searcher after new things, and sources a lot of interesting new products from the 'States in particular.
Self-restraint is almost impossible in here for cookery fiends. In fact it is completely impossible, so go on: punish that plastic.

- **OPEN:** 10am-6pm Mon-Sat (till 7pm Thu)

CITY CENTRE

LITTLE CAESAR'S PALACE
Adel Samy
Balfe Street, Dublin 2
Tel: (01) 671 8714

A boisterous place that fizzles with gung-ho energy, Little Caesar's specialises in pizzas, and specialises especially in the theatrics of spinning the tablets of dough way up in the air, catching them before they plummet to the ground, and then speedily dressing them and sliding them into the pizza oven to be cooked. Great fun. If you are twelve years old.

- **OPEN:** 12.30pm-12.30am Mon-Sun
- **AVERAGE PRICE:** Pizzas £4.50-£7.50

LORD EDWARD SEAFOOD RESTAURANT
David & Maureen Lyster
23 Christchurch Place, Dublin 8
Tel: (01) 454 2420

Thirty years young, with chef Paul Ingram here almost since the start and with other staff who have served here for more than 20 of those years, The Lord Edward is ageless, and rather refreshing for that. Prawn bisque; grilled turbot; scallops and prawns Newburg – old-style fish cookery is the speciality of this old-fashioned restaurant, a sort of gentlemen's club meets King's Inns dining room.

- **OPEN:** 12.30pm-3pm Mon-Fri, 6pm-10.45pm Mon-Sat
- **AVERAGE PRICE:** Lunch £16, Dinner £27

MAGILLS
Kim Condon
14 Clarendon Street, Dublin 2
Tel: (01) 671 3830

Kim Condon masterminds her family's vaunted deli, one of the city's great institutions. The cheese counter, the charcuterie counter, the oils and olives and breads and the whatever-it-is-you-could-possibly-need are all here, crammed into this tiny space, and served with inimitable panache by Ms Condon, a woman who knows her business inside out.

- **OPEN:** 9am-5.45pm Mon-Sat

CITY CENTRE

LA MAISON DES GOURMETS ❷
Nicolas Boutin & Olivier Quenet
15 Castle Market, Dublin 2
Tel: (01) 672 7258 Fax: 672 7258
lamaison@indigo.ie

"We want it to be just French. Not Italian! Only French," says Nicolas Boutin who, with Olivier Quenet runs the closest Dublin has to a true traiteur–boulangerie-patisserie.
Both the guys have solid French professional backgrounds and worked in Dublin in high profile restaurants, and their (pricey) cooking is uncompromised and classic: blanquette de veau, tomato farci, salmon in sorrel sauce, poulet basquaise, rabbits and snails. Along with their own brioche they sell artisan items such as craft olive oils, fleur du sel, cornichon, charcuterie and coffee. But what makes the shop special for us is the fact that they fly in Lionel Poilane's superlative sourdough bread from Paris – this alone makes La Maison an essential address. A second branch, Le Petit des Gourmets, has opened in the Epicurean Mall.

● **OPEN:** 8am-8pm Mon-Sat, 10am-3pm Sun

MARINA & JUSTIN
formerly The Farm Shop
George's Arcade, Sth Great George's Street
Dublin 2
Tel: (087) 2288 126

This is a very simple and rather lovely little stall amongst the bustling and energetic George's Street Arcade, a series of food stalls and others selling bric-a-brac which has gone from strength to strength in recent years as smart retailers and cooks such as Guy Stuart and Simon McWilliams have colonised this elegant Victorian thoroughfare between South Great George's Street and Drury Street.
Marina and Justin sell an excellent range of organic foods and more exotic specialities, but what makes the stall special is both the pristine condition of everything they sell, and also their enthusiasm and keenness and knowledge. If the name strikes you as strange, that's because they still haven't settled on a title for the stall as yet: suggestions on a postcard, anyone?

● **OPEN:** 9am-5.30pm Mon-Sat

CITY CENTRE

CAFÉ MAO
Rosie & Graham Campbell
2/3 Chatham Row, Dublin 2
Tel: (01) 670 4899

No one calls it anything other than Mao, and from the minute it opened its doors, the Campbells' funky, hip space has been the most popular addresses in town.
Kieron McGrath's cooking is a polite and very light form of fusion food which spices up some conventional ideas – Thai salmon fishcakes; chargrilled tuna with rocket and mango chilli salsa; vegetarian rice paper rolls – and fleshes this template out with classic Asianisms such as salmon ramen; udon noodles; beef juhn. Basically, it's Asia's Greatest Culinary Hits, and it is enjoyable, affordable and hugely successful.

- **OPEN:** Noon-3pm, 5.30pm-11pm Mon-Sun
- **AVERAGE PRICE:** Meals from £7

THE MERMAID CAFÉ
Ben Gorman & Mark Harrell
69/70 Dame Street, Dublin 2
Tel: (01) 670 8236

Ben Gorman and Mark Harrell's restaurant has been the cult success story of the city in the last couple of years, producing superlative cooking for the devoted bunch of movers and shakers who simply love this original, spirited and comfortable place to bits.
Why everyone loves it is easy to explain: this is perhaps the most personal and personable restaurant in the city, a place where design, music, food and service are all an expression of what these guys like to cook and what they like to listen to, in exactly the sort of space they feel comfortable eating in.
Ben Gorman's New England crab cakes are one of modern Dublin's classic dishes, but even with a simple prawn bisque, or with game cookery such as mallard with spinach, Mr Gorman shows utter control, and enviable intuition.
Marvellous music, a cult address for Sunday brunch (a meal they cook with obvious relish) and service which is amongst the finest in the city, complete a memorable and valuable experience.

- **OPEN:** 12.30pm-2.30pm, 6.30pm-10.30pm Tue-Sat
- **AVERAGE PRICE:** Lunch £10-£20, Dinner £20

CITY CENTRE

MILANO
Russell Daly
38 Dawson Street, Dublin 2
Tel: (01) 670 7744

Milano is actually a branch of the UK's Pizza Express chain, and is already expanding here as rapidly as its parent did across the water.
A very busy second branch is in Temple Bar – a very busy branch indeed – and a third branch is just across the Liffey, on Ormond Quay. As with any chain, the food is reliable, but has little explicit personality or originality.

- **OPEN:** Noon-midnight Mon-Sun
- **AVERAGE PRICE:** From £6

MITCHELL'S
Peter Dunne
21 Kildare Street, Dublin 2
Tel: (01) 676 0766

54 Glasthule Road, Sandycove, Co Dublin
Tel: (01) 230 2301

wines@mitchellandson.com
http://mitchellandson.com

Mitchell's newest shop is a valuable addition to the splendid gourmet ghetto of Glasthule, and it showcases just how hard this long-established firm has worked in recent years.
"It's not just about selling bottles of wine to people who walk in the door," they tell you, so there are wine classes and tours, leaflet drops and special offers, all the vital paraphernalia of wine selling which is properly attended to. For a firm with their long history, their willingness to extend their ambit is truly admirable.
The list for both Kildare Street and Glasthule is comprehensive and good, from Chave Hermitage and good clarets for the cubs of the Celtic Tiger, to Mommessin Burgundies and smart Californians like Ravenswood and Caymus. Whiskey lovers should on no account miss the famous – and extremely rare – Green Spot whiskey, made for Mitchell's by Irish Distillers, of which only 500 cases are produced annually – it is a superlative drink.

- **OPEN:** Glasthule: 10.30am-7pm Mon-Sat (till 8pm Fri) Kildare Street: 10.30am-5.30pm Mon-Sat

CITY CENTRE

MORELS AT STEPHEN'S HALL
Alan O'Reilly
14/17 Lower Leeson Street, Dublin 2
Tel: (01) 662 2480

An unprepossessing basement has been turned into a delightful dining room by Alan O'Reilly and his team, with big bright canvases dominating the space and contributing loads of colour. Paul O'Reilly's food is very good and very easy to enjoy – haddock with basil oil; dill marinated salmon; confit of duck with pumpkin purée – and efficient service and fine value have made this quiet and understated restaurant a great success.

- **OPEN:** 12.30pm-2pm Mon-Fri, 6.30pm-10pm Sat
- **AVERAGE PRICE:** Lunch £13.95, Dinner £21

THOMAS MULLOY
Thomas Mulloy
12 Lower Baggot Street, Dublin 2
Tel: (01) 676 6133

Mulloys is a valuable address for both the freshest wet fish and, in particular, good seasonal game.

- **OPEN:** 8.45am-5.50pm Mon-Fri, 8am-4pm Sat

MUSCAT
Brian Cornish & Bernie Doherty
64 South William Street, Dublin 2
Tel: (01) 679 7699

Brian Cornish and Bernadette Doherty run a cosy little pair of rooms, which you step down into off South William Street, with terrific assurance and skill.
This is very much a Mom 'n' Pop place, and as such is one of the cutest and most endearing addresses in the city. Janice Timothy has taken over from Seamus Commons in the kitchen, and the food always wears the pleasing, direct and persuasive manner of Mr Cornish and Ms Doherty themselves – they look after you well, and do ask to see the interesting reserve wine list.

- **OPEN:** 12.30pm-2.15pm Tue-Fri, 6pm-11pm Tue-Sat
- **AVERAGE PRICE:** Lunch £12.50, Dinner £20

CITY CENTRE

THE NATIONAL MUSEUM CAFÉ
Joe Kerrigan
Kildare Street, Dublin 2
Tel: (01) 662 1269

Joe Kerrigan's restaurant offers just the sort of food you want after a traipse around the museum: grilled chicken; Dublin coddle; good salads and sweet things with coffee.

- **OPEN:** 9am-5pm Tue-Sat, 2pm-5pm Sun
- **AVERAGE PRICE:** Meals £6

NICO'S
Emilio Graziano
53 Dame Street, Temple Bar, Dublin 2
Tel: (01) 677 3062

Nico's is best taken with a light heart and a sense of humour, which is pretty much the way the staff themselves take it. The food is enjoyable trattoria stuff - chicken cacciatore, pasta carbonara, zabaglione, the flaming sambucas - but the curious romance of the evening is what really counts. Guys! Watch out! The waiters just love to hit on your date!

- **OPEN:** 12.30pm-2.30pm Mon-Fri, 6pm-midnight Mon-Sat
- **AVERAGE PRICE:** Lunch £8, Dinner £20

NUDE ✪
Norman Hewson & David Quirke
21 Suffolk Street, Dublin 2
Tel: (01) 672 5577

A roaring success story from the day it opened, Nude fuses wraps, soups, and drinks into an irresistible combination. Norman Hewson cut his teeth in next door's Restaurant Tosca, and with the vision of David Quirke, and the planning of Freda Wolfe (now working in the Brook Lodge in Macreddin village – see Getting Away for the Weekend) they gave Dubliners something they had always wanted: smart, swiftly served food in informal surroundings, available all day long, and a vital contrast to the standard sandwich and coffee available everywhere else. They offer half a dozen soups each day, both hot and cold wraps, all the funky juices, smoothies and drinks you can name, and the sounds are hip.

- **OPEN:** 8am-10pm Mon-Sun

CITY CENTRE

NUMBER TEN RESTAURANT
Seamus Commons
Fitzwilliam Street Lower, Dublin 2
Tel: (01) 676 1367

Seamus Commons is a good cook, and one only wishes he had a better room than this cramped basement in which to exhibit the confident charm of his very polished cooking. Like a lot of young chefs, he likes a lot of flavours on a plate: fillet of cod will be accompanied by a (very good) saffron and coriander couscous, a (very good) roasted tiger prawn bisque, a splash of (very good) truffle oil and some (very good) confit of tomatoes, but the end result of putting so much together is almost self-defeating, as the mouth gets mesmerised by the fusion of flavours. Some smoked chicken and caramelised onion in filo is better, and with chargrilled fillet of beef, he shows he knows how to stand back, with a mushroom ravioli, some foie gras and a Madeira jus well-considered accompaniments. The execution is good, and a little more experience should see the over-complexity vanish. A spot of white paint and better lighting could also make the room more attractive, but this is nevertheless a serious talent, on the way to finding his signature.

- **OPEN:** 12.30pm-2pm Mon-Fri, 6.30pm-10pm Mon-Thu, 7pm-11pm Fri & Sat, 7pm-9pm Sun
- **AVERAGE PRICE:** Lunch £11-95-£14.95, Dinner £26.95

ODDBINS
Al Alpine
17 Upper Baggot Street, Dublin 4
Tel: (01) 667 3033
23 Rock Hill, Blackrock, Co Dublin
Tel: (01) 278 3844
125 Braemor Road, Churchtown,
Dublin 14
Tel: (01) 296 3111
360 Clontarf Road, Dublin 3
Tel: (01) 833 1653

The colossal corporate power of the Seagrams organisation has always given Oddbins enormous strength in depth, allowing this astute chain of wine shops, which moved over from the UK a couple of years back, the ability to endlessly introduce new wines to an already impressive list. Oddbins always backed this up with smart, savvy staff, and recent innovations have seen a delivery service which covers the

CITY CENTRE

entire country. Whilst many in the wine trade were trepidatious before they arrived, the truth of the matter is that Oddbins didn't carry all before them, as many might have expected. The great Dublin wine shops such as Searson's, McCabe's and Terroirs had already been working hard to improve their lists and their service, and they offer what Oddbins can't: individuality.

But the selection of wines is impressive, and it's fun to see how they can assemble a whole bushel of Malbecs, or do their best to make deeply unfashionable Greece fashionable for the first time in a couple of millennia. They like their wines very direct and flavourful, so you won't find subtle little wallflowers sitting on the shelves in here.

- **OPEN:** 10.30am-10.30pm Mon-Sat, 12.30pm-2pm, 4pm-10.30pm Sun (Blackrock closes 10pm)

ODEON BAR RESTAURANT
Barbara O'Riordan
57 Harcourt Street, Dublin 2
Tel: (01) 478 2088

This handsome bar and restaurant is hugely popular with the masses of office folk who work all around Harcourt Street during the week – blackened chicken; salad Nicoise; sandwiches such as cajun chicken or avocado and shrimp – and then on Sundays it runs a Sunday brunch club, with food like bruschetta; tomato and spinach tart; chargrilled chicken with rice. The room is swish, and can get mighty crowded.

- **OPEN:** 12.15pm-8.30pm Mon-Thur, till 7.30pm Fri-Sun
- **AVERAGE PRICE:** Meals £6-£7

THE OLD DUBLIN
Eamonn Walsh
90/91 Francis Street, Dublin 8
Tel: (01) 454 2028

Eamonn Walsh's restaurant is one of the senior citizens of Dublin restaurant life, but the boss runs it with a steady hand and his experience shows in everything. The food mixes classical cooking with Scandinavian elements: potato blini with gravlax; Barbary duck Helsinki; beef novgorod.

- **OPEN:** 12.30pm-2.15pm Mon-Fri, 7pm-11pm Mon-Sat
- **AVERAGE PRICE:** Lunch under £15, Dinner over £20

CITY CENTRE

THE OLD MILL
Iahcen Iouani
Merchant's Arch, Temple Bar, Dublin 2
Tel: (01) 671 9262

A simple place, upstairs at the Merchant's Arch, with enjoyable cooking in classic bistro style, and a romantic ambience.

- **OPEN:** 4.30pm-11.30pm Mon-Sat
- **AVERAGE PRICE:** Dinner over £15

CAFÉ OLE
Linda Madigan
11 Lower Liffey Street, Dublin 1
Tel: (01) 872 4348

There are folk who come into this little café every day and the pretext they use for their daily pilgrimage is that they are addicted to the sausage sandwiches. The reality is that they are addicted to the smile and the greeting and the hospitality of Ms Madigan, as well as the good sausage sandwiches.

- **OPEN:** 8am-6pm Mon-Sat
- **AVERAGE PRICE:** Lunch under £5

101 TALBOT ©
Margaret Duffy & Pascal Bradley
100-102 Talbot Street, Dublin 1
Tel: (01) 874 5011

101 is a valuable, personable, funky, fun, youthful place where Pascal Bradley dispenses wit and bonhomie and Margaret Duffy cooks delicious food, and this pair have been doing this in an area of town once regarded as little more than a dive, which makes their achievement all the greater. A slice of the true character of the city of Dublin.

- **OPEN:** 5pm-11pm Tue-Sat
- **AVERAGE PRICE:** Dinner from £16

ONE PICO
Eamonn O'Reilly
11 Upper Camden Street, Dublin 2
Tel: (01) 478 0307/478 0501

You will find some of the most intense and thought-out food in town in Eamonn O'Reilly's One Pico restaurant, at the top of Camden Street. He leaves no culinary stone unturned in

CITY CENTRE

his search for the new. Look at what he does, for example, with chicken and bacon, that old warhorse and staple of every hotel dining room. O'Reilly serves a dish of char-grilled chicken with a roast bacon mash, then adds in some roasted shallots and a morel cream. O'Reilly has the skill to make this cooking work, and all that is lacking is a more suitable space for this arch modernist.

- **OPEN:** Noon-2.30pm Mon-Fri, 6pm-10.30pm Tue-Sat
- **AVERAGE PRICE:** Lunch £12.50-£15.95, Dinner from £22

AFRICAN, HALAL & KOSHER

The following are essential stores for imported specialist foods.

AL TAYIBAT
11 Camden Street

ASIAN FOOD STORE
61 Camden Street

CHOICE'S AFRO WORLD BOUTIQUE
31 Bolton Street, Dublin 1

ERLICH'S KOSHER BUTCHER
35 Clanbrassil Street, Dublin 8

ISLAMIC CENTRE
163 South Circular Road, Dublin 8

ISLAMIC CULTURAL CENTRE
19 Roebuck Road, Clonskeagh, Dublin 14

TEKO & SONS
South Richmond Street, Dublin 8

TROPICAL SHOP
146 Parnell Street, Dublin 1
Dedicated African food shop

TROPICAL STOP CENTRE
40 Camden Street, Dublin 8

ALSO:
AFRICANA RESTAURANT
102 Parnell Street, Dublin 1
Mary Akin serves genuine African dishes.

CITY CENTRE

PANEM
Ann Murphy
21 Lower Ormond Quay, Dublin 1
Tel: (01) 872 8510

Panem's offer of good, assured, informal Italian food, and a smart, stylish place in which to enjoy it, has made this little place one of the hotspots on the north of the river. The soups are freshly made, and alongside a small selection of sandwiches they fill their own focaccia breads at lunchtime, when the other offer is a selection of pasta dishes, abetted on Thursdays by pâte di riso, where pastry wraps up ragu sauce with cheese, spinach and rice. There is a delivery service in the immediate vicinity, and here is further proof of the culinary renaissance of the northside of the Liffey.

- **OPEN:** 9am-5pm
- **AVERAGE PRICE:** Lunch from £3.50

PASTA FRESCA
Mai Frisby
3-4 Chatham Street, Dublin 2
Tel: (01) 679 2402

More than a decade on from its opening, Pasta Fresca remains a favourite haunt of many Dubliners. The shop continues out front, selling fresh pasta, oils and sauces, whilst the restaurant is open all day, selling a familiar range of pastas and Italian dishes and their own Caffe Fresca coffees.

- **OPEN:** 8am-11pm Mon-Sat, 12.30pm-8.30pm Sun
- **AVERAGE PRICE:** Meals £5-£10

PEACOCK ALLEY
Conrad Gallagher
The Fitzwilliam Hotel, St Stephen's Green,
Dublin 2
Tel: (01) 662 0760

Conrad Gallagher's career has come to resemble that of his mentor, Alain Ducasse, with whom he worked in Monte Carlo before returning to Ireland. Like Ducasse, he survived calamity – an aeroplane crash in Ducasse's case, illness in Gallagher's – and from then on has engaged in a frantic exercise of empire building, just as Ducasse has done. From his initial time in a tiny basement on Baggot Street, aston-

CITY CENTRE

ishingly only a few years ago, Gallagher now has three large city restaurants – Peacock Alley, Lloyd's Brasserie on Merrion Street and the new Ocean on Charlotte Quay, which concentrates on fish cookery, and there is also a restaurant in his native Letterkenny. A new book is about to be published as we write, his second, and Gallagher has still to hit 30.

Such empire building effectively takes Gallagher beyond the remit of the Bridgestone guides, with our concentration on individual owners and chefs, but it should be pointed out that when the man himself is at the stove, then his food is a pure thrill, brilliantly conceived and executed, marvellously original and challenging.

- **OPEN:** 12.30pm-2.30pm, 6.30pm-10.30pm Mon-Sat
- **AVERAGE PRICE:** Lunch £23, Dinner £45-£65

IL PRIMO
Dieter Bergman
16 Montague Street, Dublin 2
Tel: (01) 478 3373

A fine wine list assembled by Dieter Bergman is one of the main attractions of the intimate little Il Primo. The food is familiar modern Italian, and very popular with the local office folk who work all around here.

- **OPEN:** 12.30pm-3pm, 6pm-11pm Mon-Sat, 6pm-10pm Sun
- **AVERAGE PRICE:** Lunch under £10, Dinner from £15

QV2
John McCormack
14/15 St Andrew St, Dublin 2
Tel: (01) 677 3363

QV2 is the most stylish and enjoyable of the cluster of restaurants on St. Andrew Street, and Eoin McDonnell's food hits all the right modern buttons: rigatoni with smoked chicken, merguez and cream; scallops with spring onions and a pink grapefruit and ginger butter sauce; jerk seasoned chicken; tomato risotto with avocado enchilada and a tequila and lime dressing. Accessible and relaxed.

- **OPEN:** Noon-3pm, 6pm-12.30am Mon-Sat
- **AVERAGE PRICE:** Lunch £12, Dinner £15-£20

EPICUREAN FOOD MALL

> Situated between Middle Abbey Street and Liffey Street the Epicurean Food Mall is an exciting new development that unites talented artisans and food specialists in a handsome, welcoming mall. Further stall holders will appear in the future. The following are those in occupation as we go to press.

AROMA BISTRO & PANINIS
They serve both Irish and continental breakfasts, along with paninis with parma ham and mozzarella and other ingredients, and savoury food such as lasagne, chicken wings and salads. Tel: 01- 872 0796

THE BIG CHEESE COMPANY
A northside branch of David Brown's excellent city centre operation, this is a great location for superlative farmhouse cheeses and lots of high quality dried goods and interesting breads.

CAFFE FRESCA
An interesting little coffee shop.

CAVISTON'S SEAFOOD BAR
City centre satellite of the legendary fish shop, deli and restaurant of Glasthule on the southside. The fish counter is superb – beautiful baby squid; silver hake; wild sea bass – the smart cooking in the little café right on the money – shrimp ceviche; queen scallops with lemongrass glaze; crab claws with Asian butter (from Asian cows, perhaps?).
Tel: 01-878 2289

LA CORTE
All manner of Italian food and drink, sold with great enthusiasm.

CREME DE LA CREME
The Ouchbakou brothers make the sort of elegant patisserie which Dubliners have been deprived of for decades: Alcazar; Monte Carlo; Hedgehog, along with breads, croissants, baguettes and pain au chocolat. Tel: 01-836 4202

ISTANBUL
Alex Kartein and Okif Oztas offer real Turkish cooking, served just the way you would find it in an Istanbul lokanta. Lovely borek, lamacon, chicken donner kebabs and other epicalities, and this is the only place in Ireland to find this great cuisine. Tel: 01-878 0177

ITSABAGEL
Peaches Kemp's buzzy operation sells both plain and filled bagels and soups. The Californian has bacon, mozzarella, basil and avocado, the Gourmet Veggie has goat's cheese, roasted peppers, hummus, sundried tomato tapenade, onion marmalade and salad leaves, and everything is fizzy with flavour.

KAFFE MOKA
A buzzy little coffee house, another sister of the original branch in Rathmines.

LEYDEN'S FINE WINES
Joe Leyden developed the Epicurean Mall, and retained this unit as its flagship wine shop. The range is excellent, drawn from a dozen or more suppliers, and staff are very helpful. Tel: 01-878 2221

NATURAL FOOD PARTNERSHIP
Sean McArdle sources the produce he sells very carefully, so the various exotica you will find in this arcade stall will be unusual and top quality. Dried fruit, real Turkish delight, wild mushrooms, harissa and olives are all extremely good. Tel: 01-286 6596

THE ORGANIC SHOP
Meat from Danny O'Toole of Terenure and vegetables from Dick Wellwood are the highlights of this stall, which also has Glenisk yogurts and Drumboory goat's milk. Tel: 01-872 9411

LE PETIT DES GOURMETS
North side offshoot of the hugely successful Castle market shop, with more of the same elegant and well-achieved French cooking: gravadlax pancakes; good terrines, and the superb Poilane bread. Tel: 01-878 1133

SANDRA'S CHOICE
Sandra Carey styles her outlet as "The Store that Cares", and that care is evident in the appealing and handsome food-to-go which she prepares: Mexican chilli; roasted red pepper tart; Italian chicken; beef in Guinness; leek and Gruyere tart; potato and smoked bacon salad. Tel: 01-872 9480

SPICE OF LIFE
Lots of good spices and a torrent of international foods.

● **OPEN:** The Epicurean Food Hall is open 10am-6pm, Mon-Sat

CITY CENTRE

THE RAJDOOT TANDOORI
Ricky Singh
26-28 Clarendon Street, Dublin 2
Tel: (01) 679 4274

The Rajdoot opened at that time when Indian restaurants aimed at the upper-end of the restaurant market, before the Balti craze introduced simple food, low prices and a canteen ethic to Indian cooking. It doesn't require a second mortgage, however, to explore the delights of vegetable sashlik, channa bunna, the tandoori dishes, the splendid onion kulcha and consistently excellent vegetarian cooking.

- **OPEN:** Noon-2.30pm Mon-Sat, 6.30pm-11.30pm Mon-Sun
- **AVERAGE PRICE:** Lunch from £7, Dinner £20

RUBICON
Bruce Lavender, Susan Walsh & Gina Murphy
6 Merrion Row, Dublin 2
Tel: (01) 676 5955

This is a popular place with lots of the business folk who work around Baggot Street and The Green, who admire its good, accessible, modern cooking and sharp service.

- **OPEN:** Noon-3pm, 6pm-10pm Mon-Sun (no lunch Sun)
- **AVERAGE PRICE:** Lunch £15, Dinner £25

THE RUNNER BEAN
Mark O'Connor
4 Nassau Street, Dublin 2
Tel: (01) 679 4833

This is a reliable fruit and vegetable shop, with a large awning and trays of good things which spill out from the front door onto Nassau Street.

- **OPEN:** 7.30am-6pm Mon-Sat

SAAGAR
Sunil & Meera Kumar
16 Harcourt Street, Dublin 2
Tel: (01) 475 5060

There may not be a lot of atmosphere in this basement restaurant, at the St Stephen's Green end of Harcourt Street, but the cooking can impress — spicy hot Colombo

CITY CENTRE

fish curry; excellent tandoori chicken - and there are some novel creations of the chefs, such as murgh dumpukht, a mild chicken dish with a coconut and almond base which is sweet, nutty and delicious. The Kumars have other branches of the restaurant, in Mullingar and Athlone respectively.

- **OPEN:** 12.30pm-3pm Mon-Fri, 6pm-11.30pm Mon-Sun
- **AVERAGE PRICE:** Lunch £7, Dinner £16

SENOR SASSI'S
Ray Smyth
146 Upper Leeson Street
Dublin 4
Tel: (01) 668 4544

Various chefs have come and gone from Ray and Janice Smyth's restaurant over the years since it first opened, but it sails sublimely on irrespective of just who is manning the stoves, offering the well-heeled locals modern Irish cooking in an amiable and relaxed space.

- **OPEN:** Noon-2.30pm Thu-Fri, 6.30pm-10.45pm Mon-Sat
- **AVERAGE PRICE:** Lunch £7.50, Dinner £25

THE SHALIMAR
Anwar Aziz
17 South Gt George's Street
Dublin 2
Tel: (01) 671 0738

Shalimar has both a first-floor restaurant and a basement Balti house, which allows them to offer two variants of the Pakistani Punjab cuisine in which the restaurant specialises. The simple Balti dishes - chicken, seafood, keema, vegetable kofta, cooked, served and eaten from a karahi - are affordable and enjoyable and always well executed in the basement. Upstairs, meantime, the setting is more formal, and concentrates on classic tandoori specialities, Punjabi dishes, and some fine biryanis.

- **OPEN:** Noon-2.30pm Mon-Sat, 6pm-midnight Mon-Thu & Sun, till 1am Fri-Sat
- **AVERAGE PRICE:** Lunch under £10, Dinner from £15

CITY CENTRE

SHERIDAN'S CHEESEMONGERS
Seamus & Kevin Sheridan
11 South Anne Street
Dublin 2
Tel: (01) 679 3143

Seamus and Kevin Sheridan have been the most impressive and most dynamic people in Irish food in recent years. Beginning with a small stall in the Galway market, they paired that up with a stall in the Temple Bar market, and followed their Galway store with this lovely shop on South Anne Street. Their rise to pre-eminence has been built on the simple foundation of hard work: not only do they know their cheeses, they travel the country to work with the cheesemakers and to learn all about the individual Irish cheeses. To source their Italian specialities – terrific olive oils and the best salamis and pancetta you will find – they have established relationships in Italy (via the Slow Food movement) and travel there to make new discoveries.

The result is simple: they understand everything they sell, implicitly and precisely. Don't, for example, make the mistake of going into Sheridan's and asking for something particular: the way to get the best out of these shops is to have an open mind, and to ask: what do they recommend? If it's right and it's ready, they will tell you. Their staff are just as hip as the brothers, with Fiona Corbett running the Dublin store with great grace. Brilliant.

- **OPEN:** 9am-6pm Mon-Sat

SIMON'S PLACE
Simon McWilliams
George's Street Arcade
Dublin 2
Tel: (01) 679 7821

Simon McWilliams has been in the food business in Dublin for yonks, and his formula remains consistent and successful – big bowls of bulky soups, cheerful chunky sandwiches, hefty hunky salads – enjoyed by a young, spirited crowd.

- **OPEN:** 8.30am-6pm Mon-Sat
- **AVERAGE PRICE:** Lunch £3-£4

CITY CENTRE

SINNERS
Gerry Salaam
12 Parliament St, Temple Bar, Dublin 2
Tel: (01) 671 9345

Sinners produces friendly Middle Eastern cooking, in a friendly atmosphere, with mezzes a speciality of the house.

- **OPEN:** 5.30pm-midnight Mon-Sun
- **AVERAGE PRICE:** Dinner £15

THE STAG'S HEAD
Peter Caffrey
Dame Court, Dublin 2 Tel: (01) 679 3701

This atmospheric pub merits inclusion simply because its pub food is so consistently the best pub cooking in the city.

- **OPEN:** Pub hours

LA STAMPA
Louis Murray
35 Dawson Street, Dublin 2 Tel: (01) 677 8611

This former Guildhall is a most gorgeous room, as tall and grand as a Belle Epoque Parisian brasserie, and sometimes just as noisy. Rooms are currently being added to the complex, the owners having bought the next-door building, so La Stampa is currently in transition.

- **OPEN:** 12.30pm-2.30pm Mon-Fri, 5.30pm-midnight Mon-Fri, 6pm-12.30am Sat-Sun
- **AVERAGE PRICE:** Lunch £20, Dinner £30-£35

STEPS OF ROME
Federica Fantoro
Chatham Street, Dublin 2 Tel: (01) 670 5630

This is everybody's favourite little pizza place, it seems, and the veritable definition of a cult address, The Steps of Rome is just a single room with a counter, beside Neary's pub, and folk just love it. The pizzas, especially the potato and rosemary, are widely admired, whilst the warm nonchalance of the service is darling. Analyse it bit by bit and it doesn't seem much. But allow it to weave its spell, and you can't resist it.

- **OPEN:** 10am-11pm Mon-Sun
- **AVERAGE PRICE:** Meals £5

CITY CENTRE

SUPPER'S READY
Eric Tydgadt & Kevin Daly
51 Pleasants Street, Dublin 8
Tel: (01) 475 4556

Classic food home-delivery dinner service for CCTT ("can't cook too tired') city dwellers — onion soup; boeuf bourguignon; navarin of lamb; lemon tart; chocolate mousse.

● **NOTES:** Minimum order is £5, delivery charge is 70p, and there is a wine list also. Phone for details

SWEENEY O'ROURKE
Shane & John O'Rourke
34 Pearse Street, Dublin 2
Tel: (01) 677 7212

This shop supplies mainly to the trade, but ordinary decent folk can stroll in and splash out on Global knives and good saucepans and everything the kitchen needs. Do check out the really smart lampshades (not for sale, unfortunately).

● **OPEN:** 9am-5pm Mon-Fri

THE TEA ROOMS ●
Michael Martin
6-8 Wellington Quay, Dublin 2
Tel: (01) 670 7766

Michael Martin has one of the most beautiful rooms in the city to work in, and he congratulates his setting with cooking that is measured, thoughtful and hugely enjoyable; the Tea Rooms is a hot destination. Whilst his cooking is as Mediterranean-modern as anyone's, there is a lot of signature style to his work — salad of lamb and pecorino, with a walnut and lime vinaigrette; sirloin of beef with foie gras croute and an anchovy and black pepper dressing; roast salted cod with a risotto of cep and rocket; roast veal with brandade of potato and cabbage; caramelised peach with rice pudding tart. Martin likes warm, elemental flavours, which makes his food extremely easy to enjoy. The room is very well run and is exceptionally handsome, and the gin martinis are easily the best in the city.

● **OPEN:** 12.30pm-2.15pm Mon-Fri, 6.30pm-10.10pm Mon-Sat, 6.30pm-10pm Sun
● **AVERAGE PRICE:** Lunch £13.50-£17, Dinner £30

CITY CENTRE

TOSCA
Norman Hewson
20 Suffolk Street, Dublin 2
Tel: (01) 679 6744

Norman Hewson's atmospheric room, with Geoff O'Toole cooking clever modern food is just the right mix for the lean space of Tosca.

- **OPEN:** 12.30pm-5.30pm, 6.30pm-11pm Mon-Sun
- **AVERAGE PRICE:** Lunch £6-£10, Dinner £16

TRASTEVERE
Giovanni Cafolla
Temple Bar Square, Dublin 2
Tel: (01) 670 8343

Lots of glass and a Temple Bar Square location make this a good spot for watching the world and its wife go by. The food is standard Irish-Italian, and not without its moments.

- **OPEN:** 12.30pm-11pm Mon-Sun
- **AVERAGE PRICE:** Lunch under £10, Dinner £16

TROCADERO
Rhona Teehan & Robert Doggett
3 St Andrew's Street, Dublin 2
Tel: (01) 677 5545

The legendary Frank, head waiter for decades in the Troc, is now tending tables in some other celestial realm, but even without him, the Troc (you always call it the Troc, by the way) remains a timeless womb of good times. There is nowhere like the 'Troc, and few other places in the city provoke the affection in which this restaurant is held.
The food is straight out of the 1960s, and sometimes it can seem that the food is almost out of the 1860's, but who notices? And anyway, who the hell cares? Certainly not the night owls, thespians, hacks and media-movers who are devoted to this noble institution and who patronise it faithfully. You can't be a true citizen of Dublin until you have eaten and drunk (too much, far too much) in the Troc.

- **OPEN:** 6pm-12.15am Mon-Sat
- **AVERAGE PRICE:** Dinner £20

CITY CENTRE

TULSI
Bablu
17A Lower Baggot Street, Dublin 2
Tel: (01) 676 4578

The enormous menu, offering twenty starters to begin with and no fewer than ten poultry dishes, may be unprepossessing, but the team at Tulsi works hard and is very concerned that you should enjoy this little restaurant, even down to offering to cook things not on the menu should you request them. There is a take-away branch on Olive Mount Terrace, Dundrum Road, Dublin 14, Tel: (01) 260 1940

- **OPEN:** Noon-2.30pm, 6pm-11.30pm
Mon-Sat, 6pm-11.30pm Sun
- **AVERAGE PRICE:** Lunch £6-8, Dinner £10

UNICORN RESTAURANT
Giorgio Casari
Merrion Court, Merrion Row, Dublin 2
Tel: (01) 676 2182

The Unicorn's food is a very curious tratt-meets-bistro fare - chowder; baked haddock with aubergine; a buffet from which you can choose a selection of cold dishes and meats - but, truth be told, the appeal of the the Unicorn is not its food. The appeal is the crowd, and there are few better entertainments in the city than this fizzy mix of wannabees, politicos and media folk, all eyeing each other up.

- **OPEN:** 12.30pm-3pm, 6pm-11.30pm Mon-Sat,
till midnight Fri-Sat
- **AVERAGE PRICE:** Lunch £10, Dinner £15

VAUGHAN JOHNSON
11 East Essex Street, Temple Bar, Dublin 2
Tel: (01) 617 5355

Dublin branch of the well-regarded Cape Town wine shop which specialises in South African wines. They offer varietals from more than 30 S.A. winemakers, as well as their own Vaughan Johnson range, alongside international wines sourced from Irish suppliers

- **OPEN:** 11am-9.30pm Mon-Sat, 10.30am-9pm Sun

DUBLINER'S CHOICE

MIKE O'TOOLE'S FIVE ESSENTIAL ADDRESSES

1

THE MORRISON
great coffee and cool New York-style hotel

2

LA MAISON DES GOURMETS
for bread

3

THE METRO, SOUTH WILLIAM STREET
best tuna melts

4

ARTHOUSE, TEMPLE BAR
combines art/technology and coffee house

5

SHERIDAN'S CHEESEMONGERS
plain good service

Mike O'Toole is Ireland's leading food photographer

CITY CENTRE

VELURE BAR & RESTAURANT
Jean-Francois Delaunay
47 South William Street, Dublin 2
Tel: (01) 670 5585

Velure is the latest restaurant incarnation for this long, lean room on South William Street, and the modern, knowing design is matched by modern food: crushed potatoes; braised veal with root vegetables; lots of Mediterranean flavourings and stylings. At weekends they serve what they call a Linner (cross between Lunch and Dinner) between 3pm-6pm.

- **OPEN:** 5.30pm-10.30pm Mon-Thur, Linner 3pm-6pm Fri & Sat
- **AVERAGE PRICE:** Meals from £20

AR VICOLETTO
Luigi Fantoro
5 Crow Street, Temple Bar, Dublin 2
Tel: (01) 670 8662

This is a cute little trattoria with food that can be flavourful and good fun, if a little unreliable. They stick to tratt classics – beef Ar Vicolette; veal with wine sauce; crostini with anchovies; spaghetti with mussels and tomatoes.

- **OPEN:** Noon-4pm, 6pm-11.30pm Mon-Sat, 2pm-11.30pm Sun
- **AVERAGE PRICE:** Lunch from £10, Dinner from £17

WAGAMAMA
Norma Kennedy
South King Street, Dublin 2
Tel: (01) 478 2152

The first Wagamama outside London is housed in a calm room, with lighting which is nothing less than masterly. The food is familiar – noodles, rice dishes, fruit and vegetable juices and beers – but it is well delivered and it seems to us that the noodles here are infinitely better than those served in the London branches. Interestingly, the early concentration on Zen and wisdom and all that "Way of the Noodle" stuff, so prevalent when the Wagamamas first opened, seems to have been forgotten. Pity. There is definitely something spiritual about a perfect bowl of soba noodles.

- **OPEN:** Noon-11pm Sun-Thu, noon-midnight Fri-Sat
- **AVERAGE PRICE:** Meals £10

CITY CENTRE

WINDING STAIR BOOKSHOP & CAFÉ
Kevin Connolly
40 Lower Ormond Quay, Dublin 1
Tel: (01) 873 3292

This unique address offers excellent daytime food, a perfect complement to the browsing calm and sassy alternativism of this lovely bookshop, easily the most beautiful bookshop-and-café in the city. Other bookshops have cafés, but none have the character or atmosphere of the Winding Stair.

- **OPEN:** 10am-6pm Mon-Sat, 1pm-6pm Sun
- **AVERAGE PRICE:** Lunch £2-£5 (evening opening planned)

YAMAMORI NOODLES
Niall Carey
71 South Gt George's Street, Dublin 2
Tel: (01) 475 5001

The Yamamori has an ever-increasing stream of devotees who love its noodles, and its hipness and its cheapness. The music is fabulous, the Japanese waitresses splendid, and Yoshi Iwasaki's cooking is buzzy with flavour, the flavours well expressed in dishes such as soba noodles with chicken and spring onion, or udon noodles with seaweed and vegetables. Good punchy flavours and good value.

- **OPEN:** Noon-5.30pm, 5.30pm-11pm Mon-Sat, 4pm-11pm Sun
- **AVERAGE PRICE:** Meals £12-£18

ZAFRAAN
Simon Siew
41 South Great George's Street, Dublin 2
Tel: (01) 677 0999

Zafraan serves what we might call new wave Indian and Asian fusion food, which sounds impossibly eclectic, but can enjoy some fine successes, such as poitin-scented rice pancakes; crisp-fried lamb with onion and soya; wild mushrooms with cumin-scented cottage cheese; tiger prawn curry with green mango, even a blackcurrant ragout with those tiger prawns. Challenging.

- **OPEN:** 12.30pm-2.20pm, 5.30pm-11pm Mon-Sun
- **AVERAGE PRICE:** Lunch £7.95, Dinner £15

THE DUBLIN PUB

For decades, Dublin's pubs remained the same – small, smoky, intimate, reliable as a faithful dog. Then, all of a sudden, glitzy new mega pubs, which can accommodate zillions of drinkers, opened up. Old timers won't be seen in these places, of course, which are largely the preserve of the youthful quaffer.

More importantly, however, for the serious drinker, has been the opening of a small scattering of brew pubs. First amongst these in the city was The Porterhouse, on Parliament Street, followed by the small bar at the Dublin Brewing Company, where Liam McKenna (no relation, unfortunately) brews the finest beers in the country. Messrs Maguire at O'Connell Bridge quickly followed, and it is a true treat to try all their different brews, for these people are serious about the business of brewing, a direct contrast to the big-scale brewers whose drinks seem to us to disimprove year by year.

The following are a selection of the most interesting Dublin pubs, arranged in three sections: Brew Pubs, Classic Pubs and The New Wave.

BREW PUBS

■ DUBLIN BREWING COMPANY
North King Street, Smithfield, D7
The bar is open to visitors during office hours and groups can be accommodated by telephoning in advance (01- 872 8622). They produce some awesome brews: Beckett's Gold; D'Arcy's Dublin Stout; Maeve's Crystal Ale (our favourite); Revolution Ale. All must be tried, and there are some interesting fruit beers in development.

■ MESSRS MAGUIRE
Burgh Quay, D2
A great big pub with good brews: Plain and Extra Stout; Haus pilsner; Yankee lager; and Rusty, a red ale which is the one we like best.

■ THE PORTERHOUSE
Parliament Street, D2
Peter Mosley makes 8 brews for this fine pub, all the way from pilsner style Temple Brau (ho, ho) to the classic Oyster Stout, Wrasseler XXXX and the stonking An Brianblasta, a merciless 7% ABV.

CLASSIC PUBS

■ THE BAILEY
2 Duke Street, D2
Stylish pub, which spills out onto the street in summertime.

■ THE BRAZEN HEAD
20 Lower Bridge Street, D8
Very popular with tourists.

■ DAVY BYRNE'S
21 Duke Street, D2
Leopold Bloom's pub, eternally.

■ THE DOCKER'S
Sir John Rogerson's Quay, D2
U2 love it, everyone loves it.

■ DOHENY & NESBITT'S
5 Lower Baggot St, D2
Barristers love it, everyone loves it.

■ THE DUKE
9 Duke Street, D2
A real classic.

■ FALLON'S
The Coombe, D8
Classic pub, cool crowd.

■ FOX'S FAMOUS SEAFOOD KITCHEN
Glencullen, Co Dublin
Raucous at times, but some may find it a bit Oirish and designed for tourists.

■ GROGAN'S CASTLE LOUNGE
South William St, D2
Enduring and endearing.

■ THE HORSESHOE BAR
The Shelbourne Hotel
St Stephen's Green, D2
The true seat of the Irish Government.

■ THE INTERNATIONAL BAR
23 Wicklow Street, D2
Pull that pint for us one more time, Simon.

■ KAVANAGH'S
Prospect Square, Glasnevin, D9
Known as The Gravediggers, and ever unchanging.

■ KEHOE'S
9 South Anne St, D2
Cramped, crowded, classic.

THE DUBLIN PUB

■ **KENNY'S**
Lincoln Place, D2
Part and parcel of Trinity College life.

■ **THE LONG HALL**
51 Great George's Street, D2
One of the most beautiful bars in the city.

■ **McDAID'S**
3 Harry Street, D 2
Heaven for literary tourists.

■ **MULLIGAN'S**
8 Poolbeg Street, D2
The best pint of stout in the city? Maybe.

■ **NEARY'S**
1 Chatham Street, D2
Theatrical and comfortable.

■ **O'DONOGHUE'S**
15 Merrion Row, D 2
Music lover's heaven.

■ **THE PALACE**
21 Fleet Street, D2
One of the finest traditional pubs.

■ **RYAN'S**
28 Parkgate Street, D8
A beautiful pub, down by the Phoenix Park.

■ **SHEEHAN'S**
17 Chatham Street, Dublin 2
Interesting crowd and good drinks.

■ **SLATTERY'S**
29 Capel Street, D1
For music heads, a key address.

■ **STAG'S HEAD**
1 Dame Court, D 2
The best pub food in town, and good pints.

■ **TONER'S**
139 Lower Baggot Street, Dublin 2
Hacks and hackettes haunt the place.

NEW WAVE PUBS

■ **CAFÉ EN SEINE**
40 Dawson Street, D2
Fin de siecle Paris in start-of-the-century Dublin.

■ THE FRONT LOUNGE
Parliament Street, D2
Suave and stylish – the Wallpaper* crowd would drink here.

■ OCTAGON BAR
The Clarence Hotel, D2
Great cocktails, high prices, noisy air conditioning.

■ THE CHOCOLATE BAR
Harcourt Street, D2
As cool as it gets, with exotic loos as well.

■ THE GLOBE
Great George's Street, D2
Very trendy young crowd.

■ HOGAN'S
George's Street, D2
Nicely understated made-over pub.

■ LIFE CAFÉ-BAR
Abbey Life Mall, Middle Abbey Street, D1
Sofas and lots of minimalist style.

■ THE NORSEMAN
29 East Essex Street, D2
One of the hippest Temple Bar pubs.

■ ODEON
Harcourt Street, D2
Sunday brunch with the papers is the best time.

■ PRAVDA
Liffey Street, D1
Great design, thunderous crowd.

■ THOMAS READ
Parliament Street, D2
A fry-up, a weekend pint and the Weekend paper sections.

■ THE TEMPLE BAR
Temple Bar, D2
Hugely popular, and has a beer garden for the fine weather (what fine weather?)

■ THE TURK'S HEAD
Parliament Street, D2
We knew it before it was fashionable.

■ ZANZIBAR
Ormond Quay Lower, D1
A truly gargantuan, miles-over-the-top boozer with lots of palm trees.

SOUTHSIDE ● BALLSBRIDGE

BALLSBRIDGE

BATTS
Leonie Guy
10 Baggot Lane, Dublin 4
Tel: (01) 660 0363

Leonie Guy's restaurant has been restyled, but her cooking remains as consistently correct as ever: Caesar's salad with garlic croutons; brandied chicken liver pate; rack of lamb with mustard and herb crust; duck breast with potato and parsnip rosti. Excellent value, and valuably unpretentious.

- **OPEN:** 10am-10pm Mon-Fri (lunch noon-3pm), 6pm-10pm Sat
- **AVERAGE PRICE:** Lunch from £8, Dinner £15-£20

BELLA CUBA
Akim Beskri
11 Ballsbridge Terrace, Ballsbridge
Tel: (01) 660 5539

This upstairs room has transmuted through a number of identities in recent years, but Bella Cuba looks like it might have found the formula to attract an audience.

- **OPEN:** 12.30pm-2.30pm, 6pm-11pm Mon-Sun
- **AVERAGE PRICE:** Lunch £10.50, Dinner £20

LE COQ HARDI
John Howard
35 Pembroke Road, Dublin 4
Tel: (01) 668 4130/668 9070

2000 will be the last year for John and Catherine Howard's restaurant, Le Coq Hardi, as the owners prepare to put their feet up and take it easy at the end of the year, having sold the building. Mr Howard has been one of the great Dublin restaurateurs, his cooking always appropriate and superbly understood, and he has also been one of the fathers of modern Irish cooking, having started to use Irish artisan ingredients long before it ever became fashionable. We shall not see the likes of the Coq again, more's the pity.

- **OPEN:** 12.30pm-2.30pm Mon-Fri, 7pm-11pm Mon-Sat
- **AVERAGE PRICE:** Lunch £24, Dinner from £35

SOUTHSIDE ● BALLSBRIDGE

EXPRESSO BAR
Ann Marie Nohl
1 St. Mary's Road, Ballsbridge, Dublin 4
Tel: (01) 660 0585

They do things well in The Expresso, which explains why this cool room is so popular. Grilled haddock with a rosemary mash and Mediterranean vegetables is just the sort of thing that shows their capabilities, mixing the prosaic with the obvious in a successful union, largely thanks to the fact that they care about the food and getting it right. The room will be largely filled with twenty-something business girls at lunchtime, smart women who know a good thing when they eat it, and the weekend brunch crowd are a stylish bunch.

● **OPEN:** St Mary's Road: 7.30am-11.30am breakfast, noon-5pm lunch Mon-Fri, 6pm-9.30pm Tue-Sat, 9am-5.30pm, 6pm-9.30pm Sat, 10am-5.30pm Sun
● **AVERAGE PRICE:** Brunch £4-£5, Lunch £8-£10, Dinner £15

FITZERS CAFÉS
Frank & Gerry Fitzpatrick
50 Dawson Street, Dublin 2 Tel: (01) 677 1155
Temple Bar Square, Dublin 2 Tel: (01) 679 0440
National Gallery, Merrion Square, Dublin 2
Tel: (01) 661 5133

The Dublin rooms of the Fitzers group are startlingly diverse: funky in Temple Bar, serene in the National Gallery, and laid back on Dawson Street. The cooking is as modern as you would expect, but can tend to rely on assembling ingredients rather than convincing you with creativity.

● **OPEN:** Temple Bar: noon-11.30pm Mon-Sun; Dawson Street: (9am-11.30pm); National Gallery: 9am-5pm Mon-Sat (till 8pm Thur)

GOURMET FRANCE
Christopher & Hugh Logue
49 Waterloo Road, Dublin 4
Tel: (01) 667 4712

GF specialises in foods from south west France, principally foie gras in multifarious forms, but also high quality smoked duck, dried mushrooms, truffle oil and chestnuts. Sourcing is very careful, so quality is high, and there are fine hampers.

● **OPEN:** Telephone for further details

SOUTHSIDE ● BALLSBRIDGE

THE GOOD FOOD STORE
Vanessa Clarke
7 Pembroke Lane, Dublin 4
Tel: (01) 667 5656

Everything about Vanessa Clarke's lovely little shop speaks of good choice, of a clear vision on the part of the owner. Ms Clarke sells only organically produced food – lovely vegetables from Denis Healy of Wicklow; Holyhill butter from Cork; fresh eggs; farmhouse cheeses; organic milk and dairy products; olives; cured meats – but what makes The Good Food Store even more special is the simple, unflustered air of the shop, such a tender antidote to the overheated experience that is shopping in supermarkets. It is, in many ways, like a Continental shop, loosely structured, elegant, wise, and its mix of foods-to-go (all of them excellent), smart sandwiches at lunchtime (join the queue!) and essential comestibles make it a joyful place in which to shop.

● **OPEN:** Open 9am-7.00pm Mon-Fri, 9am- 5.30pm Sat

HEMINGWAYS OF BALLSBRIDGE
Adrienne McCrory
2a Merrion Road, Ballsbridge
Tel: (01) 668 9550

This is a very popular place at lunchtime, when local office workers create a huge queue to buy lunchtime food to go, and for the rest of the day Adrienne prepares very classic dinner food – boeuf bourguignonne; coq au vin; salmon en croute; a selection of good salads.

● **OPEN:** 10am-7pm Mon-Fri, 9.30am-6pm Sat

HIBERNIAN HOTEL
David Butt
The Patrick Kavanagh Room
Eastmoreland Place, Dublin 4
Tel: (01) 668 7666 Fax: 660 2655

Raphael Delage has succeeded the excellent David Foley in the kitchen of the excellent Hibernian, having worked as his second chef for some time, so consistency can be expected.

● **OPEN:** all year, lunch & dinner open to non-residents Mon-Sat
● **AVERAGE PRICE:** B&B £150-£185, Dinner £30

SOUTHSIDE ● BALLSBRIDGE

LOBSTER POT RESTAURANT
Tommy Crean
9 Ballsbridge Terrace, Dublin 4
Tel: (01) 668 0025/660 9170

There must be something about fish cookery which inspires a loveable culinary conservatism, for The Lobster Pot, like the Lord Edward or Howth's King Sitric or Skerries' Red Bank, is an ageless, changeless place.
The cooking is straightforward cordon bleu, which means they show you the fish, then take it away, cook it and match it with lots of butter and cream and booze. And it is quite lovely, food you can never tire of, and it is quite pricey. And again, like the other ageless fish restaurants, service is only excellent.

● **OPEN:** 12.30pm-2.30pm Mon-Fri, 6.30pm-10pm Mon-Sat
● **AVERAGE PRICE:** Lunch £25, Dinner £25-£30

O'CONNELL'S ●
Tom O'Connell, Aileen Murphy
Bewley's Aparthotel, Merrion Road
Ballsbridge
Tel: (01) 647 3400 Fax: 647 3499
oconnells@bewleyshotel.com

O'Connell's has been a smash hit since the day it opened its doors, with Aileen Murphy's cooking proving to be deliciously irresistible. Tom O' Connell oversees the room – which is housed in the Bewley's Aparthotel but is actually a separate venture – with considerable assurance, and the cooking – right from the popular breakfasts through to dinner – is delivered with panache: leek and smoked salmon tart; pizzetta with spinach, tomato and ewe's milk cheese; sirloin of beef with horseradish; superb carrageen moss pudding.
The room itself is a little disparate, but very comfortable, and it changes very well from breakfast – always very good – through to dinner. Service and value are both very keen. There are plans to create a new first-floor restaurant, with the original O'Connell's complementing it as a brasserie. O'Connell's is a model of professionalism, and this is one of the hottest destinations in the city.

● **OPEN:** 7am-10am, 12.30pm-2pm (1pm-4pm Sun), 6pm-10pm Mon-Sun
● **AVERAGE PRICE:** Lunch £12.50, Dinner under £20

SOUTHSIDE • BALLSBRIDGE

ROLY'S BISTRO
Colin O'Daly
7 Ballsbridge Terrace, Dublin 4
Tel: (01) 668 2611

Roly's is nowadays a transatlantic operation, with a Stateside branch in Palm Beach Gardens, Florida (tel: 561 694 0066). Now that, as William Faulkner might have said, is rather a long way to go for dinner, so thank heavens the Ballsbridge Roly's sails on as graciously as ever.

The big upstairs room is light and rumbustious (though some find it does get a little loud when full, and it is usually full), and whilst there can be an unevenness because of the large numbers ("every night is Saturday night at Roly's") you can still enjoy food here from head chef Paul Cartwright which manages simple perfection, especially with the well-established dishes such as the splendid bisque, the Kerry lamb pie, Dublin Bay prawns with garlic, chilli and lemon.

Like everyone, we miss the presence of Roly Saul, one of the founders, but, truth be told, Roly's always achieves something special: the commingling of food, wine, craic, service, value and style into a spiffing experience.

- **OPEN:** Noon-3pm, 6pm-10pm Mon-Sun
- **AVERAGE PRICE:** Lunch £12.50, Dinner £16-£25

BLACKROCK

AYUMI-YA ©
Yoichi Hoashi
Newpark Centre, Newtownpark Avenue, Blackrock
Tel: (01) 283 1767
info@ayumiya.ie   http://www.ayumiya.ie

The Japanese food in Ayumi-Ya is impressively well understood and delivered, and as its Dublin customers have become more adventurous over the years the restaurant has been allowed to play to its strengths, serving raw yellowfin tuna as part of a tantalising, yet restorative plate of San Francisco sashimi, as well as the easily loved tempura; soba noodles with chicken and the ever present miso soup. Great service, and there is also a small shop selling Japanese foods.

- **OPEN:** 6pm-11pm Mon-Sat, 5.30pm-9.45pm Sun
- **AVERAGE PRICE:** Dinner over £20

SOUTHSIDE ● BLACKROCK

BLUEBERRY'S
John Dunne & Stephane Couzy
15 Main Street, Blackrock
Tel: (01) 278 8900

Owned by the team who make Morels in Glasthule such a success – chef John Dunne and front-of-house Stephane Couzy – Blueberry's has been Blackrock's hot spot in recent times. David Grossiere has succeeded Michael Rath in the kitchen, and if the food lacks the earthy oomph! which made Blueberry's name, it is nevertheless very moreish: sea bass with asparagus and beurre blanc sauce with a helping of pepperonata; marinated tuna with char-grilled potatoes, cumin and coriander; excellent nougatine crème brulée; great almond biscotti with blueberries. What is constant, however, is the fact that the room is quite lovely, service is right on the money and prices are very fair. The only trouble is that it can be hard to get a table in this very happening place.

● **OPEN:** 12.30pm-2.15pm Mon-Fri, 5.30pm-10pm ('till 10.30pm Fri 6pm-10pm Sat) 12.30pm-3pm, 6pm-9pm Sun
● **AVERAGE PRICE:** Lunch £10.95-£13.95, Dinner from £24

BURGUNDY DIRECT
Conor Richardson
8 Monaloe Way, Blackrock
Tel: (01) 289 6615 burgundy@indigo.ie

Smashing small firm that specialises in excellent wines from Burgundy, from small producers, abetted by some rare Italian wines.

● **OPEN:** Telephone for a list and delivery details

BUTLER'S PANTRY
Eileen Bergin
53 Mount Merrion Avenue Tel: (01) 288 3443
97b Morehampton Rd, D'brook tel: (01) 660 8490

Eileen Bergin's ever-reliable traiteur, Butlers Pantry, was amongst the first of Dublin's cooked food shops, and it remains one of the best, with good breads, well made soups, enjoyable main dishes and creamy desserts that you simply never tire of eating. Helpful and thoughtful service complete a successful equation. There is a second branch of Butler's Pantry on Morehampton Road in Donnybrook.

● **OPEN:** 9.30am-9pm Mon-Sat, 11am-3pm Sun

SOUTHSIDE ● BLACKROCK

CAKES & CO
Joannie Langbroek, Leslie Keogh & Rosanna Mulligan
25 Rock Hill, Blackrock Village
Tel: (01) 283 6544 Fax: 280 4861
ventur24@indigo.ie

Sugarcraft is a dazzling, arcane skill, and the cakes produced by the girls at Cakes & Co are as dazzling as it gets, extraordinary inventions in sugar which delight and amaze with their expertise and their intricacy. You simply cannot have a special celebration without a themed cake from Cakes & Co. And don't think it's all about appearances: these cakes are for eating and seriously enjoying.

● **OPEN:** 9.30am-6pm Mon-Fri, 9.30am-5pm Sun

DALI'S
63-65 Main Street, Blackrock
Tel: (01) 278 0660

A modern room, with light, modern-food.

● **OPEN:** Noon-3pm, 6pm-10.30pm Tue-Sat
● **AVERAGE PRICE:** Lunch £9, Dinner £20

McCABE'S WINE MERCHANTS ●
Jim McCabe
51-55 Mount Merrion Avenue, Blackrock
Tel: (01) 288 2037 Fax: 288 3447
value@mccabes

Jim McCabe's shop boasts not just one of the biggest ranges of wines sold in Ireland, but also a terrifically stylish shop with superb staff, a fine wine club, and many enjoyable and provocative tastings. While other merchants stood still during the 1990's, McCabe's powered ahead with a refitted shop, creating a truly glamorous space where it is a pleasure to browse and buy.
Like the best wine merchants, Jim McCabe and his team understand that the customer these days doesn't just want a bottle to drink, they want to access the entire culture of the world of wine. And that is what you are offered here, along with an exhaustive range of wines and spirits, in one of the city's great shops.

● **OPEN:** 10.30am-10pm Mon-Sat, 12.30pm-2pm, 4pm-10pm Sun

SOUTHSIDE ● BLACKROCK

THE OLIVE TREE
Bahaa Jaafai
22 Newtownpark Avenue, Blackrock
Tel: (01) 278 0933

Bahaa Jaafai, fondly regarded for his work in La Tavola in Booterstown has opened this mix and match of Eastern Mediterranean, Greek, Cypriot and Arabic cooking in the Olive Tree. "I want to cook all the most popular dishes of this region – which include humus, lamb kebabs, falafel, taramasalata... and even the pastas from the South of Italy which show Arabic influences."
An Egyptian, trained in France by Italians, who first worked with Greeks, Bahaa is fluent in all these complementary cuisines.

- **OPEN:** 6pm-11pm Tue-Sat
- **AVERAGE PRICE:** Dinner £15-£24

RISTORANTE DA ROBERTA
Roberto Morsiani
5 George's Avenue, Blackrock
Tel: (01) 278 0759

Somewhat grander in style than most of the city's Italian restaurants, Roberto Morsiani opened up in Blackrock after making a good name in Ashford, in County Wicklow. The food has an enviable ambition, but the restaurant really succeeds as a good-night-out location, with a lively crowd and a good buzz proving just as important as the food.

- **OPEN:** 5.30pm-11.30pm Tue-Sat, 1pm-10pm Sun
- **AVERAGE PRICE:** Dinner £15-£20

LA TAVOLA
Kevin Hart & Phillip Davis
114 Rock Road, Booterstown
Tel: (01) 283 5101

The former chef and front of house of La Tavola have bought over this very popular roadside restaurant, and continue the tradition of good pasta and pizza cookery begun by Bahaa Jaafai, who has moved further south to Blackrock, to The Olive Tree.

- **OPEN:** 5pm-11.30pm Tue-Sat
- **AVERAGE PRICE:** Dinner under £20

COFFEE SHOPS

Dublin has gone crazy over coffee in recent years, and the opening of new coffee houses seems unstoppable. New names such as Perks and Insomnia are opening throughout the city, and no one will bet you a penny to a pound that Starbucks, the US chain, won't be making its way to the city soon.

If Dublin has coffee houses, what it lacks is baristas, those magical artists of the Barilla (average age in Italy, 47 years!) who are born to produce an espresso which expresses all the glory of coffee. In Dublin, a lot of the espressos made are indifferent, and sometimes downright bad, so you need to choose carefully. The following are some favourite places.

BREWBAKER'S
22 South Frederick Street, Dublin 2
Tel: (01) 677 8288
Well regarded cup of coffee.

BROWN'S BAR
Brown Thomas, Grafton St, Dublin 2
Tel: (01) 679 5666
The chic Brown's Bar, downstairs in chic Brown Thomas, also offers a menu of soups, sarnies, salads and drinks. The loos are terrifically convenient for Grafton Street shoppers.

BUTLER'S CHOCOLATE CAFÉ
Wicklow Street
The company also has a chocolate shop at the top of Grafton Street.

CAFÉ INN
6 Parliament Street, Dublin 2
Tel: (01) 679 3398
The Inn has an excellent range of teas and coffees.

CAFÉ IRIE
11 Upper Fownes Street, Temple Bar, Dublin 2
Popular left-field sort of spot.

CAFÉ JAVA
145 Upper Leeson Street, D 4 Tel: (01) 660 0675
5 South Anne Street, Dublin 2 Tel: (01) 660 8899
Popular breakfast, lunchtime and coffee-time places.

CHOMPY'S
Powerscourt Centre, Dublin 2
Tel: (01) 679 4552

& CAFES

The great American breakfast is one of the big attractions in Frank Zimmer's popular place.

THE COFFEE CLUB
4 Haddington Road, Dublin 4
Tel: (01) 667 5522
Along with good coffees and teas they take great pride in their sandwiches in this likable coffee bar.

GLORIA JEAN'S COFFEE CO
Powerscourt Townhouse, Dublin 2
Tel: (01) 679 7772
Gloria Jean's offers an enormous array of coffees, all from Arabica beans, and a range of flavoured coffees. You can drink them here, or buy the coffees and whatnot to go.

HARVEY'S COFFEE HOUSE
Trinity Street
Eternally popular, especially for breakfast.

INSOMNIA COFFEE COMPANY
6 White Friars, Aungier Street, Dublin 2
www.insomnia.ie
Derek Hughes' smart cafés (the second branch is on the main street in Blackrock, the third in The Pavilion in Dun Laoghaire on the southside) play terrifically groovy music and have a true seriousness about the business of coffee. Look out for their Frappachillo, a sweet, cold blast of coffee.

JOY OF COFFEE
25 East Essex Street, Dublin 2
Tel: (01) 679 3393
A nice, comfy café with good coffee and a range of photographs which you can buy.

QUEEN OF TARTS
Cork Hill, Dublin 2
Tel: (01) 670 7499
Excellent cakes and coffees and good savoury baking have made the Queen something of a cult success.

WEST COAST COFFEE COMPANY
Lincoln Place & Camden Street

THE WINDING STAIR
40 Lower Ormond Quay, Dublin 1
Tel: (01) 873 3292
The classic bookshop-café.

SOUTHSIDE ● BLACKROCK

VALENTIA COOKERY
Linda Booth
25 Avoca Park, Blackrock
Tel: (01) 278 2365

Linda Booth runs a much admired cookery school, with an excellent range of specialist classes and some very interesting guest chefs demonstrating during the season.

- **OPEN:** Telephone for course details and a brochure.

CABINTEELY

RODNEY'S BISTRO
Rodney & Deirdre Doyle
Cabinteely Village
Tel: (01) 285 1664

There are some well executed dishes to be enjoyed in this intimate little restaurant – rosti fishcake with chilli, ginger and coriander; lamb's kidneys with Meaux mustard; Thai-style cod wrapped in filo; desserts such as baked lemon tart or Bailey's mousse. It's far from the cutting edge, and locals like it just like that.

- **OPEN:** from 7pm Tue-Sat
- **AVERAGE PRICE:** Dinner £15-£20

DALKEY

AL MINAR
Mr Rahlman
21 Castle Street, Dalkey
Tel: (01) 285 0552

A quiet little Indian restaurant on the main street of the village of Dalkey, quietly lit, with quiet service, the Al Minar makes up for this deference by enjoying the demands of customers who ask for dishes to be prepared in the way the staff eat them.

- **OPEN:** Noon-11.30pm Mon-Sat, 6pm-midnight Mon-Sun
- **AVERAGE PRICE:** Lunch under £10, Dinner over £15

SOUTHSIDE ● DALKEY

DANIEL FINNEGAN
Paul Finnegan
2 Sorrento Road, Dalkey
Tel: (01) 285 8505

Finnegans is a fine old pub, and the food is well above the norm, with the seafood reason alone to trek up the hill. Do note that it can be very busy indeed at lunchtimes, so it can be advisable to try to book a table.

● **OPEN:** 12.30pm-3pm Mon-Fri, 12.30pm-2.30pm Sat

DON GIOVANNIS
Farzad
25 Castle Street, Dalkey
Tel: (01) 284 9550

The essential little, local Italian place, always welcoming.

● **OPEN:** 5.30pm-10.30pm Mon-Thu
● **AVERAGE PRICE:** Dinner £15

MUNKBERRY'S
Chris Bailie
Castle Street, Dalkey
Tel: (01) 284 7185

Chris Bailie's cooking is ambitious, complex and very tall, and whilst he can sometimes lose the logic of a dish, there are fine details in his work and the room itself is beautiful.

● **OPEN:** 5.30pm-10pm Mon-Sat
● **AVERAGE PRICE:** Lunch from £19

ON THE GRAPEVINE
Pamela Cooney
St. Patrick's Road, Dalkey
Tel: (01) 235 3054

Pamela Cooney's shop was inspired by the superlative Terroirs wineshop in Donnybrook, and it is a rather special and thoughtful shop, stylishly decorated and designed, and with both an excellent selection of wines and some fine specialist foods to complement the choice bottles.

● **OPEN:** 11am-8pm Mon-Sun (till 9pm Fri & Sat)

SOUTHSIDE ● DALKEY

THE QUEEN'S/THE VICO
Andrew Neiland
Castle Street, Dalkey
Tel: (01) 285 4569

There are two restaurants in this handsome and hugely popular old pub on the main street of Dalkey. The Vico is upstairs and is more formal, mixing linen service with a char grill and a piano bar. La Romana downstairs offers zappy pastas and pizzas in a room beside the bar. The bar itself serves bar lunch and evening "bar bites" which are scrummy and popular – crab crostini; steak sandwich; a daily pasta dish.

- **OPEN:** The Vico: 6pm-11.30pm Mon-Sat, 12.30pm-10pm Sun, La Romana: 6pm-11.30pm Mon-Sun, The Queen's serves food: noon-5pm Mon-Sun, "bar bites" 6pm-8pm.
- **AVERAGE PRICE:** The Vico: from £20; La Romana: £10-£15

RAGAZZI
Fabio Perrozzi
109 Colimore Rd, Dalkey
Tel: (01) 284 7280

Ragazzi is the happening restaurant in Dalkey, beloved of the girls on a big night out thanks largely to the Italian (male) waiters. "They love women – so don't go there for a romantic evening!" said a – recently engaged – female friend.
Ragazzi is the sort of place that you will remember visiting for years to come, but chances are you will forget completely what you ate or drank when you went there – you just remember the good time you had, and that's important.

- **OPEN:** 5.45pm-10.30pm Mon-Sat, 4.30pm-10.30pm Sun
- **AVERAGE PRICE:** Dinner £15-£20

ROSSINI'S
Yvonne Dolan & Orla Webb
14 Castle Street, Dalkey
Tel: (01) 284 7184

"A good shop, and getting better" is how Rossini's is described locally. They stock well chosen items such as the Guy Stuart range and such fashionable favourites as semi-dried tomatoes. At the back of the store is a lovely wine shop which is perfect for browsing and buying.

- **OPEN:** 9am-6pm Mon-Fri, 9am-5.30pm, 12.30pm-3.30pm (Sun open summer only)

SOUTHSIDE ● DALKEY

THAI HOUSE
Tony Ecock
21 Railway Road, Dalkey
Tel: (01) 284 7304

This fine restaurant boasts an enviable culinary reputation, created by Tony Ecock and by the late and much-missed Boonma Nilrat.

- **OPEN:** 6pm-midnight Tue-Sun
- **AVERAGE PRICE:** Dinner under £20

P. D.'S WOODHOUSE
Helen Argyle & Peter White
1 Coliemore Road, Dalkey
Tel: (01) 2849399

PD's Woodhouse has carved out a neat niche for itself as a place to feast on good char-grilled steaks - this is their speciality - baked potatoes and crisp salads.

- **OPEN:** 6pm-11pm Mon-Sat, 4pm-9.30pm Sun
- **AVERAGE PRICE:** Dinner £15-£22

DONNYBROOK

DOUGLAS FOOD CO.
Grainne Murphy
53 Donnybrook Road, Dublin 4
Tel: (01) 269 4066

Grainne Murphy spent time working in the food business in the 'States and she has brought a very sharply focused idea of customer service to the splendid operation that is the Douglas Food Co.
"We aim to take the chore out of preparing and cooking food so that all our customer has to do is enjoy it," says Grainne, so the shop offers an interesting assortment of classics – chicken jardiniere terrine; Chinese sesame pork; chocolate marquis – which in turn is supplemented by a range of specialist foods "from mini blinis to Wahini rice to Brie de Meaux". Quality is always high, and this is one of the city's finest traiteurs.

- **OPEN:** 10am-7.30pm Mon-Fri, 9.30am-6pm Sat, 11am-6pm Sun

SOUTHSIDE ● DONNYBROOK

ERNIE'S
The Evans family
Mulberry Gardens, Donnybrook,
Dublin 4
Tel: (01) 269 3260

Set in a courtyard just off the main strip of Donnybrook (and rather hard to find, to tell you the truth), Ernie's is a pampering little place, characterised by a true, old-fashioned dedication to service. The food has nothing to do with fashion - rack of Wicklow lamb with Madeira; lamb's liver with sage; guinea fowl with Puy lentils; prune and Armagnac tart - and that is just how the older crowd who eat here like it.

- **OPEN:** 12.30pm-2pm Tue-Fri, 7.30pm-10.30pm Tue-Sat
- **AVERAGE PRICE:** Lunch £14.95, Dinner £25

ROY FOX ●
Des Donnelly
49a Main Street, Donnybrook,
Dublin 4
Tel: (01) 269 2892

This extraordinary shop is truly a cornucopia of good things. Into a tiny space, up a little laneway off the main strip of Donnybrook, Des Donnelly has managed to line up what seems like the entire world of food in one single place.
There is nothing you cannot get here: smoked garlic; mooli; grilled Sicilian aubergine; country buttermilk; cassia bark; cooked polenta; Brittany crepes. Everything. "I never try and define what we are," says Des, but that's because Roy Fox is really a hypermarket meets a bazaar meets a souk someplace in Dublin 4, and then some more.
The energy in this shop, particularly on Sunday afternoons, is only awesome. This is one of the finest shops in the city.

- **OPEN:** 9am-7pm Mon-Sun

FURAMA CHINESE RESTAURANT
Rodney Mak
88 Donnybrook Road, Dublin 4
Tel: (01) 283 0522

Furama is a Chinese restaurant which makes the minimum of culinary compromises for its clientele, which allows chef Freddie Lee to produce food that is always interesting.

SOUTHSIDE • DONNYBROOK

There are, of course, lots of standard items on the menu, but it is the more unusual dishes that are most exciting: black sole drunken style; king prawn in minced pork; green pepper with prawn stuffing; roasted crispy belly pork.

- **OPEN:** 12.30pm-2pm, 6pm-11.30pm Mon-Sat (Fri & Sat till midnight), 1.30pm-11pm Sun
- **AVERAGE PRICE:** Lunch over £10, Dinner £22

MOLLOY'S OF DONNYBROOK
Donnybrook Road, Dublin 4
Tel: (01) 269 1678

This is a fine shop for both fresh fish and game, and also for cooked fish dishes.

- **OPEN:** 8.45am-6pm Mon-Sat (till 4pm Sat)

O'BRIENS FINE WINES
Brendan O'Brien
30-32 Donnybrook Road, Dublin 4
Tel: (01) 269 3033

This fast-expanding chain has its newest branches at Blackrock and Rathmines as well as the Maple Centre on the Navan Road, joining their long-established shops in Bray and Greystones, Dun Laoghaire and Dalkey, Donnybrook, Sandymount, Rathgar and Stillorgan. They are agents for a wide range of wines, beers and spirits, the newest arrivals being the Australian Tatachilla range.

- **OPEN:** 10.30am-11pm Mon-Sat, 12.30pm-2pm, 4pm-11pm Sun

TERROIRS ©
Sean & Françoise Gilley
103 Morehampton Road, Dublin 4
Tel: (01) 667 1311 Fax: 667 1312

Sean and Françoise Gilley run what is perhaps the most interesting wine shop in the city. Beautifully designed and arranged, Terroirs is home to a fabulous selection of wines. But the shop is truly made special by Françoise Gilley's beautiful window arrangements, and also by her meticulous eye for sourcing specialist French foods – this is a place in which

SOUTHSIDE ● DONNYBROOK

to find the most fantastic chocolates (they are agents for the superlative Valrhona), olive oils and mustards, coffees and teas and other artisan foods from France, gorgeous things which cannot be found anywhere else in Ireland, as well as the very best bottles from all over the globe. There really is nowhere else like Terroirs, and do note that they are good at finding rare vintages for birthdays and anniversaries.

● **OPEN:** 10.30am-8pm Mon-Sat

DUN LAOGHAIRE
THE BOMBAY PANTRY
Ronan Fleming & Vivek Sahni
Glenageary Shopping Centre, Glenageary
Tel: (01) 285 6683

There are many southsiders who insist that not only does the Bombay Pantry do the best take-away food in the city, but that it actually cooks the best Indian food found anywhere in town. Trying some of the gorgeous, perfectly understood cooking of Vivek Sahni and Ronan Fleming, it can be hard to disagree. These guys are terrifically good at what they do, and superlatively confident, and a meal bought from the Bombay Pantry is no mere take-away: it is a treat. Their samosas – stuffed with potato, peas and peanuts – are spot on, the batata vada – a potato dumpling stuffed with cashews, peanuts and lemon, coated in a gram batter – is another excellent starter, and their chicken karahi is the best on the block, a perfectly executed meld of tomatoes, peppers, chillies, fenugreek and coriander which is the best we have eaten outside of Pakistan. Breads and all the other details are splendid, and the Pantry is a joy.

● **OPEN:** Noon-11pm Mon-Sat, 5pm-10.30pm Sun.
Delivery service 6pm-11pm in a 3-4 mile radius
● **AVERAGE PRICE:** Meals £8-£10

BRASSERIE NA MARA
Shanta Chowdree
The Harbour, Dun Laoghaire
Tel: (01) 280 6767 Fax: 284 4649

Paul Keogh's cooking in the stylish Brasserie is very modern: gravadlax with a buckwheat blini and coriander cream;

SOUTHSIDE ● DUN LAOGHAIRE

rillette of duck and foie gras; deep-fried hake in a tortilla crust – served in a delightful, modern room.

- **OPEN:** 12.30pm-2.30pm, 6.30pm-10pm
- **AVERAGE PRICE:** Lunch over £20, Dinner over £30

CAVISTON'S
Peter & Stephen Caviston
59 Glasthule Road, Sandycove
Tel: (01) 280 9120 Fax: 284 4054
caviston@indigo.ie http://indigo.ie/~caviston/

Delicatessen: If it's good, then it will find its way to Caviston's, Stephen and Peter Caviston's remarkable deli, which is one of the icons of Irish food. This is one of the great fun places to shop, a treasure trove of the best Irish artisan foods and the best fish counter in the city. Queue up to buy some fish, and by the time you have decided what it is you want, Peter Caviston will have entertained and educated you and everyone else royally, with gossip and anecdote and craic and conjecture. First time we ever came in here, we left with a recipe for onion sauce to complement our fish, and it was every bit as good as Peter Caviston told us it would be. Elsewhere, the deli sells MacNean soups and stocks, buckets of olives, excellent fresh leaves and herbs, their own salads and pates and meats, and a kaleidoscope of good things: Copsewood yogurts; Torc truffles; Stone Oven breads; Kilmurry preserves; Glenisk organic milk; almost all of the Irish farmhouse cheeses. The staff echo Stephen and Peter to the note, and there is nowhere else quite like it.

Restaurant: Noel Cusack knows exactly what he can do, knows the best way to do it, and he does it that way each and every day for his devoted customers. They pack three lunchtime sittings into this little room, contented southsiders who know that this fish cookery cannot be bettered. The discipline and inventiveness of Cusack and his little team is inspiring, their cooking utterly spiffing: salad of Boston shrimps; squid with olive oil and garlic; chargrilled swordfish with mojo picon, and there are also some vegetarian choices such as blue cheese soufflé or ragout of vegetables with herbs. Happily for city centre folk, there is a new Caviston's fish bar and counter in the Epicurean Food Mall, Liffey St.

- **OPEN:** Shop open 9am-7pm Mon-Sat; Restaurant open three sittings per day: noon-1.30pm, 1.30pm-3pm, 3pm-3.45pm Tue-Fri; noon-1.45pm, 1.45pm-3.15pm, 3.15pm-3.45pm Sat
- **AVERAGE PRICE:** Meals £15-£20

DUBLINER'S CHOICE

GARY JOYCE'S FIVE ESSENTIAL ADDRESSES

❶
AVOCA HANDWEAVERS

Kilmacanogue and Powerscourt.
Well worth going out of your way for. Great home cooking and wonderful surroundings. Excellent staff, and service with a smile, no matter how busy. Good for families, and tempting after-meal shopping too!

❷
MORTON'S

Still the classic family-run small supermarket. They have everything you need if you're interested in good quality fresh food, with the same faces behind the counters and checkouts for years. They know most of their customers by name, and you can even have an account.

❸
ROY FOX

An old fashioned vegetable wholesalers, with a vast range of food ingredients, fresh cheeses, olives, breads and hard-to-find foods.
Open 7 days a week.

❹
AYA

An original concept, very well executed. Not too purist, so they even have a weekend brunch menu for those of us who enjoy a traditional Irish.

❺
NECTAR

Freshly made juices, salads, mains and wraps for the masses, and good coffee too. Queues out the door at weekends. Staff with great attitude.

Gary Joyce is Director of Genesis Corporation

SOUTHSIDE ● DUN LAOGHAIRE

HICK'S BUTCHERS
Ed Hick
Woodpark, Sallynoggin, Dun Laoghaire
Tel: (01) 285 4430

The finest pork butcher in the country, no less. See the entry for Ed Hick under the Temple Bar Market.

● **OPEN:** 8.30am-5.30pm Tue-Fri, closed 1pm-2pm

MOREL'S BISTRO
John Dunne & Stephan Couzy
18 Glasthule Road, Dun Laoghaire
Tel: (01) 230 0210

The great success story of the southside, chef John Dunne and host Stephan Couzy run a superb restaurant, which has quickly spawned a sister restaurant in the shape of Blackrock's Blueberrys. There is no mystery as to why Dunne and Couzy make such a good team and create such a good restaurant. They keep their menu restricted to dishes they can accomplish with skill and consistency – magnificent duck confit; deep-fried brill with herb mash; mussel soup with saffron; beef fillet with shallots; prawn risotto with saffron and fennel; tian of dark chocolate and mint – they create an ageless bistro ambience night after night, and they have a smart wine list at smart prices. Excellent.

● **OPEN:** 5.30pm-9.45pm Mon-Fri, 6.30pm-10.30pm Sat, 12.30pm-3pm, 6pm-9pm Sun
● **AVERAGE PRICE:** Sun Lunch £13.50, Dinner from £25

O'TOOLE'S BUTCHERS
Tom O'Connor
1b Glasthule Road, Dun Laoghaire
Tel: (01) 284 1125

The southside outpost of Danny O'Toole's indispensable butcher's shop is run by Tom O'Connor, who genially and graciously manages a shop that sells organic meat of the most superlative quality. Everything is as good as everything else, so the pork and bacon are true flavoured and delicious, and the beef is as good as it gets. Mr O'Connor is patient, helpful and skilful, and his knowledge completes the equation of a butcher's shop which is exemplary.

● **OPEN:** 8.30am-6pm Mon-Sat (half day Mon, closed 12.30pm)

FOXROCK

BISTRO ONE
Mark Shannon
Foxrock Village, Dublin 18
Tel: (01) 289 7711

Set upstairs over a dry cleaner's shop in this little commercial strip of Foxrock village, Bistro One is proof that Foxrock folk can be trusted to keep a secret, for Mark Shannon's restaurant is just about the best-kept food secret on the southside. The neat one page menu offers smart cooking – starters such as duck confit with Roquefort; smokies; spinach and parmesan tart; a selection of pastas as either starters or main courses, and ruddy main courses – lamb shank with rosemary; crispy duck with potato and apricot stuffing; Bistro One's Irish stew; fillet steak with garlic butter – and there are daily specials and excellent desserts. Bistro One is truly a comfort zone, with an open fire, good cooking, and a brace of regulars who return again and again.

- **OPEN:** 7pm-10.30pm Tue-Sat
- **AVERAGE PRICE:** Dinner from £20

THOMAS' DELICATESSEN
Thomas Murphy
4 Brighton Road, Foxrock, Co Dublin
Tel: (01) 289 4101

Thomas's is an excellent deli, with all the select foods one expects from a thoughtful owner, and the wine section of the shop is particularly impressive, with its main strength directed towards the French wines the locals appreciate. Good service and good wine advice are extra elements.

- **OPEN:** 8am-7.30pm Mon-Sat, 8am-3pm Sun

GOATSTOWN

THE OLIVE TREE
Ibrahim Phelan
Islamic Centre, Roebuck Road
Tel: (01) 260 3721/260 3740

There is both a restaurant and shop in the Islamic Centre, offering Middle Eastern food – baba ghanoush; hummous;

SOUTHSIDE • GOATSTOWN

tabbouleh, spicy chicken curries, couscous with lamb. Everything is offered at astonishingly low prices – which makes it popular with students from UCD as well as locals.

- **OPEN:** Noon-8pm Mon-Sun
- **AVERAGE PRICE:** Meals £3-£4.50

DUBLIN CHIP SHOPS

Most of the Italian families who run chip shops in Ireland come from Casalatico, which is north of Naples and south of Rome. Today, they still produce some of the best chips and fish suppers you can buy, and like the great Dublin chipper, Burdock's, many of them are legends in their own dinnertime.

Here are some good ones:

C. APRILE
10 Kilmacud Road, Stillorgan

BENNY'S FISH & CHIPS
Parnell Street

BESHOFF BROTHER'S
Harbour Road, Howth (also Clontarf)

BORZA'S
Sandymount Green

CAFE ANGELO
36 Wexford Street, Dublin 2

CAFFOLA'S
75 Mespil Road

FUSCIARDI'S
10 Capel Street, Dublin 1

SOUTHSIDE ● MONKSTOWN

MONKSTOWN

THE PURTY KITCHEN
Old Dunleary Road
Monkstown
Tel: (01) 284 3576

A very popular pub with well-regarded pub cooking.

● **OPEN:** Pub hours

SEARSON'S
Charles Searson
Monkstown Crescent
Tel: (01) 280 0405 Fax: 280 4771

Charles and Frank Searson's business has emerged as the finest wine merchant in the city in recent years, their range of wines steadily extending to include smashing new arrivals from Spain and some other fine French regional wines which complement some of the great French regionals they already stock, such as Cuvée Mythique and Chateau St. Auriol.
They were fortunate to hit upon the brilliant Con Class wines from Rueda – the sauvignon blanc is one of the best value wines you will find – and all told these are exciting times for a very individualistic wine merchant. Their En Primeur offers are exceptionally thoroughly researched and described by Frank Searson, and their delivery service throughout the country is excellent and very efficient.

● **OPEN:** Open 10.30am-7pm Mon-Wed, 10.30am-9pm Thur-Fri, 10.30am-7pm Sat

VALPARAISO
Con Galligan
99 Monkstown Road
Monkstown
Tel & Fax: (01) 280 1992

Spanish colourings of vivid blue and yellow, and Spanish accented food - tapas, gambas al ajillo, piperade - are the recipe of the long-established Valparaiso.

● **OPEN:** 6pm-11pm Mon-Sat, 5pm-10pm Sun
● **AVERAGE PRICE:** Meals from £12

DUBLINER'S CHOICE

TOM DOORLEYS FIVE (IN FACT SIX) ESSENTIAL ADDRESSES

❶ BALLYCUMBER MEATS

Dun Laoghaire Shopping Centre: because their beef and lamb is naturally reared on their own farm in the Midlands and never fails to taste great.

❷ CAVISTON'S

for the best fish, good cheese, great banter and because you meet everybody there on a Saturday morning (and what a place for lunch!)

❸ CP HACKETT

of Capel Street, because if you can't be bothered to organise your vegetable garden in good time they stock plants of leeks, cabbages, sprouts, cauliflower, lettuce, purple sprouting broccoli and more.

❹ BLOOMFIELD'S

Dun Laoghaire, because as supermarkets go this is probably the best and it stocks a great range of cheese and plenty of organic meat, fruit and veg.

❺ THE PORTERHOUSE

Parliament Street, because I just don't like big brand beer and far prefer an occasional Wrassler's XXXX or, titter ye not, a Bishop's Finger.

❻ THE WINDING STAIR

because I love secondhand bookshops and when you add good, wholesome grub, it's an irresistible combination (if they could provide deep, hot baths it would be even better).

Tom Doorley is wine and restaurant writer for The Sunday Tribune

SOUTHSIDE ● PORTOBELLO

PORTOBELLO

BRETZEL KOSHER BAKERY
Morgan Hackett
1a Lennox Street, Portobello
Dublin 8
Tel: (01) 475 2724

Nothing changes in the Bretzel, thanks heavens. The tomatoey pizza slices, the light onion breads, the gingerbread men, the sticky custards, the eternal breads, are now – and likely ever shall be – reliable, fun food.

● **OPEN:** 9.15am-5.30pm Mon-Sat, 9am-1.30pm Sun

LOCKS
Claire Douglas
Windsor Terrace, Portobello
Dublin 8
Tel: (01) 454 3391

One of the most professional and well-loved restaurants in the city, Claire Douglas runs Locks with a precision and prescience which always impresses. It is a commodious room, always character-ful, and the subtle, traditional French-style cooking is much enjoyed by the professionals who eat here, and have been eating here for years.

● **OPEN:** 12.30pm-2pm Mon-Fri, 7.15pm-11pm Mon-Sat
● **AVERAGE PRICE:** Lunch under £20, Dinner £30

PAD THAI
Fon Spaulding
Richmond Street, Portobello, Dublin 8
Tel: (01) 475 5551

A funky room with loud music and, when the diminutive Fon is in the kitchen, some snappy and fun Thai cooking: hot and sour clear prawn soup; hot peppers stuffed with tofu, nuts, coriander and corn; chicken with chilli and cashew nuts. A good hanging out spot.

● **OPEN:** 6pm-11pm Mon-Sat, 12.30pm-3pm,
Wed-Fri, 6pm-10pm Sun
● **AVERAGE PRICE:** Lunch over £10, Dinner over £15

SOUTHSIDE • PORTOBELLO

THORNTON'S
Kevin Thornon
1 Portobello Road, Dublin 8
Tel: (01) 454 9067
thorntons@iol.ie

Stuck in a traffic jam one time on the road across the canal from Kevin Thornton's restaurant, we watched through the window of the restaurant as a waiter painstakingly, patiently, rigorously and lovingly polished a big white plate with a gleaming white cloth. It was a standard moment in any restaurant as prep is under way, but somehow it seemed to us that it summed up everything about this noble restaurant, a place where every detail is considered, worked on, polished until perfection, and then worked on some more just in case they can get it better.

Kevin Thornton and his team don't follow any food fashions, and it was his time in France which really set the foundation for his future work. Certain modern touches are used, such as a soy and ginger vinaigrette with a confit of salmon served with a basil purée, or that ginger and soya used with confit of rabbit, for example – but for the most part this cooking adds a southern French touch to a rigorously controlled classical cooking in which technique is superlative: terrine of guinea fowl and baby vegetables with gazpacho sauce; roast scallops with ratatouille and a truffle sabayon; roast suckling pig with apple galette and poitin jus. Desserts are statements of the discipline: millefeuille of fresh fig with fig ice cream; bittersweet chocolate mousse with mango. Thornton's is intense, expensive, and polished to perfection.

- **OPEN:** 12.30pm-1.45pm Fri, 7pm-10.30pm Tue-Sat
- **AVERAGE PRICE:** Lunch £22, Dinner from £3

RANELAGH

BEST OF ITALY
Catriona Norton
37 Dunville Avenue, Ranelagh
Tel: (01) 497 3411 Fax: 450 4889

Recently madeover into a stylish Italian deli, Best of Italy has lots of essential Italian staples – dried pastas, risotto rice, you name it – and some interesting wines, along with cheeses and cooked meats.

- **OPEN:** 9am-7.30pm Mon-Sat, 10am-5pm Sun

SOUTHSIDE ● RANELAGH

DUNVILLE PLACE
Mick Duignan
Dunville Avenue, Ranelagh, Dublin 6
Tel: (01) 496 8181

Locally known as Dunville Palace, as it is so difficult to get a table. This snappy restaurant walks a modernist track — beef tostados with guacamole followed by brochettes of lamb with spiced couscous are typical — and there are few modern culinary gestures which Mick Duignan and his team can't concoct. Service is sharp, value is good.

● **OPEN:** 10.30am-3pm Sun-Mon, 10.30am-3pm,
6.30pm-11pm Tue-Sat
● **AVERAGE PRICE:** Lunch & Sunday Brunch £11, Dinner £30

GAMMELLS
Chris Brandan
33 Ranelagh Village, Dublin 6
Tel: (01) 496 2311

A staple of Ranelagh, with lots of good foods.

● **OPEN:** 8.30am-8pm Mon-Sun

KEEGAN'S OF RANELAGH
47 Ranelagh Village
Tel: (01) 497 1314

There are too-few shops like Keegan's left in the city, places where they remember your name, where they present and display their fish and their fruit and vegetables with care.

● **OPEN:** 9am-6pm Tue-Sat

NECTAR JUICE BAR
Chris Keegan
53 Ranelagh Village, Dublin 6
Tel: (01) 491 0934

It tells you just how old we are when we tell you that we used to come to this address to do our laundry! Chris Keegan has restyled the old Red Spot launderette as a hip juice bar with good food and excellent juices. Excellent.

● **OPEN:** 9.30am-10.30pm Mon-Fri, 10am-10.30pm Sat,
10.15am-4pm Sun
● **AVERAGE PRICE:** Lunch £5, Dinner £7

SOUTHSIDE ● RANELAGH

PRONTO
Shane Kenny
65 Ranelagh Village, Dublin 6
Tel: (01) 497 4174

Young Shane Kenny has steered the Pronto in a radically different direction from the steady path it occupied for the last forty years. Previously an amiable grills-and-chips and good-food-and-plenty-of-it place which was extremely popular with the bedsit classes of the neighbourhood, it now serves things such as seared tuna with sesame seeds, or tofu spring roll, or pesto oil with risotto. Blimey! Local wisdom tends to stick with the simpler dishes.

- **OPEN:** 11am-10.30pm Mon-Fri (till 1pm Fri-Sat)
- **AVERAGE PRICE:** Lunch £10.50, Dinner £20

PUNJAB BALTI HOUSE
Mohammed Latif
15 Ranelagh Village, Dublin 6
Tel: (01) 497 9420

Whilst described as a Balti house, the menu in this popular spot in Ranelagh village actually includes many familiar dishes - tandoori and tikka chicken, rogan josh, dansak - with the decisive accent of flavouring firmly on the Punjabi Pakistani style. Service is excellent, and their bring-your-own-wine policy means that an evening in the Punjab Balti House can be very inexpensive.

- **OPEN:** Noon-2pm Wed-Fri, 6pm-11.30pm Mon-Sun
- **AVERAGE PRICE:** Lunch under £10, dinner under £20

REDMONDS
Jimmy Redmond
25 Ranelagh Village, Dublin 6
Tel: (01) 496 0552

Jimmy Redmond's wine shop is a real treat, whether you are hunting down something special as a present or just grabbing and fast-chilling a bottle or two to take along to a nearby Balti house. Wines, spirits and beers are all well chosen, and don't neglect the good things in the shop while you are there.

- **OPEN:** 10.30am-11pm Mon-Sat, 12.30pm-2pm, 4pm-9pm Sun

DUBLINER'S CHOICE

MAURICE EARL'S FIVE ESSENTIAL ADDRESSES

(1)

HARVEY'S
Trinity Street: Best coffee in town.

(2)

TEMPLE BAR FOOD MARKET
Great food from organic vegetables to mini quiches.

(3)

THE FRONT LOUNGE
A good pint, comfortable sofas and no bric a brac nailed to the wall.

(4)

EPICUREAN FOOD MALL
If you want something decent to take home after a day's work this is the place to get it.

(5)

CORNUCOPIA
Still serving great soups and salads after all these years.

Maurice Earls runs Books Upstairs

SOUTHSIDE ● RATHGAR

RATHGAR

BIJOU BISTRO
Mark & Linda Smith
47 Highfield Road, Rathgar, Dublin 6
Tel: (01) 496 1518

This is a very popular room, with the comfortable and confident ladies of Terenure packing the place at lunchtime, and whilst one might say the cooking could do with a little more oomph! when it comes to delivering on flavour, the smart mixture of light salads and main courses is a formula that clearly works well.

- **OPEN:** 10am-3pm, 5.30pm-10.30pm Mon-Sat (till 11pm Fri & Sat), 12.30pm-10.30pm Sun
- **AVERAGE PRICE:** Lunch under £15, Dinner from £20

THE GOURMET STORE
Thomas Cronin
Rathgar, Dublin 6
Tel: (01) 497 0365

Creative and attractive window decorations signal an interesting and highly unusual shop, selling quality dried foods, good wines and deli specialities.

- **OPEN:** 9am-7pm Mon-Sat

POPPADOM
Nisheeth Tak
91a Rathgar Road, Dublin 6
Tel: (01) 490 2383

Nisheeth Tak's elegant restaurant offers the most highly regarded Indian cooking in the city, and for once here is ethnic cooking that excites because of a genuine sense of creativity and exploration. Goat's cheese fondue on taftaan bread; crab cakes with ginger and spring onions, Charminar lamb, superlative naan breads of every type are just some of the details of a original venture.

- **OPEN:** 6pm-midnight Mon-Sun
- **AVERAGE PRICE:** Dinner from £25

SOUTHSIDE • RATHGAR

THE VINTRY
Evelyn Jones
102 Rathgar Road, Dublin 6
Tel: (01) 490 5477

Evelyn Jones' shop is one of the best independent wine merchants, able from a modest premises to offer not just excellent bottles, but also a wine club — with tastings and lectures for quaffers, and they also offer a gift service and a full party service. This is a shop with true individuality.

- **OPEN:** 10.30am-10.30pm Mon-Sun. Wine club meets monthly

RATHMINES

CARMINES
Alan O'Reilly
Charleville Hotel, Rathmines, Dublin 6
Tel: (01) 496 8046

Part of the Charleville Hotel, this smart venture is run by Alan O'Reilly, one of the most perspicacious restaurateurs at work today. His formula here has been to concentrate on pasta and pizzas, but he has worked out his style exactingly, so the pizzas are thin-based and crisp, the flavourings judged just right, and the other foods wear their influences proudly — Union Square chowder, Dean & DeLuca buffalo wings — and are expertly delivered. The wine list is short and choice.

- **OPEN:** 12.30pm-10pm Mon-Sun
- **AVERAGE PRICE:** Lunch under £10, Dinner under £20

CREMA
Terry & Addrianna Fitzgerald
312 Lower Rathmines Road, Dublin 6
Tel: (01) 496 5555

A genuine family operation with sister and brother in the kitchen and out front, and parents running a bakery out back. The restaurant serves American-influenced food: scrambled egg burrito, bacon potato hash, refried bean and cheese burrito, The menu is 70% vegetarian, with especially fine soups. "Soup you could die for" they claim, and their loyal customers agree with them. Terrific service.

- **OPEN:** 8am-6pm Mon-Fri, 9am-6pm Sat
- **AVERAGE PRICE:** Lunch under £10

SOUTHSIDE ● RATHMINES

DEVENEY'S OFF LICENCE
Martin Deveney
16 Upper Rathmines Road, Dublin 6
Tel: (01) 497 2392

This popular shop also has branches at Dundrum, Sandyford Shopping Centre and Rosemount Shopping Centre, Rathfarnham.

● **OPEN:** 10.30am-11.30pm Mon-Sat (till 11pm Sun)

FOTHERGILL'S ©
Terry & Breda Lilburn
141 Upper Rathmines Road,
Dublin 6
Tel: (01) 496 2511

Few things in life are certain, but one of life's certainties is that there will always, but always, be a queue in Terry and Breda Lilburn's lovely deli, Fothergill's. Every time you come in here, a lengthy line of food lovers is lined up in the narrow shop, patiently waiting their turn. It's been like this for 15 years now.
One can also predict with certainty that you will join the queue, agonise about what to buy as you stand in line with all the other Dublin 6 folk, and then buy far, far more than you ever intended: smoked salmon quiche; lamb meatballs with Mediterranean vegetables; raspberry bombe; linzer torte. The secret of the place is the fact that it's not in the slightest bit slick. Instead, these genuine people cook genuine food.

● **OPEN:** 9.30am-6pm Mon & Sat, 9am-6.30pm Tue-Fri

THE GOURMET GALLERY
Paul Swords
306-308 Lower Rathmines Road,
Dublin 6
Tel: (01) 497 7101

Paul Swords' background in catering has given the Gourmet Gallery a self-sufficiency in terms of food production which is admirable – 90% of what they sell here they make themselves.
Working with his team of chefs, Swords prepares a daily hot lunch as well as roasting his own meats – honeyglazed ham;

SOUTHSIDE • RATHMINES

stuffed turkeys; roast beef; lemon chicken – and cooking staples such as poached salmon, beef wellington; pork with apricots, their own pates, quiches, pies and salads.
The shop stocks some excellent food lines and don't miss the mighty Spanish wines he brings in from Rafael Alvarez of Waterford. The combination of cooked food both to eat and to take away is just the right mix for Rathmines.

- **OPEN:** 9am-7pm Mon-Sat, noon-5pm Sun

MORTON'S
Alan Morton
15 Dunville Avenue, Rathmines,
Dublin 6
Tel: (01) 497 1254

The gorgeous, 1960's facade which blessed Morton's with one of Dublin's finest shopfronts has been changed, sadly, and instead of a quintessential piece of modernism, one now has a facade which is merely grand, and rather overdone.
There have been changes inside too, and the shop has concentrated increasingly on the food-to-go prepared in its own kitchen, where you can see the cooks at work. There are still many, many good things for sale, and Morton's retains its stature as one of the best, most individual supermarkets in the city: look out for the good wine counter, Marc Michel organics, and a good meat and poultry counter. Staff are relaxed and charming.

- **OPEN:** 9am-6.30pm Mon-Sat

ZEN CHINESE RESTAURANT
Denis O'Connor
89 Upper Rathmines Road,
Dublin 6
Tel: (01) 497 9428

Irish-owned, and located in an old church hall, Zen is unlike any other Chinese restaurant in the city – not an inch of lacquer anywhere. The food is also a step up from the standard offerings of so many places, and can show some real imagination.

- **OPEN:** 12.30pm-2pm, 6pm-11pm Mon-Sun
- **AVERAGE PRICE:** Lunch £10, Dinner £20

DUBLINER'S CHOICE

LEANNE DE CERBO'S FIVE ESSENTIAL ADDRESSES

❶

LOBO IN THE MORRISON HOTEL
At the moment it's easy to book a table within a day or two. There is a good atmosphere, great music and it's comfortable.

❷

BROOK LODGE AND THEIR RESTAURANT THE STRAWBERRY TREE
I like the way they've decorated the place, it's unique. And they've done it all themselves. There's no fuss and all the ingredients they use are organic.

❸

THE COMMONS RESTAURANT
It's just like, the best, isn't it. The food is superb, the staff are incredibly lovely. A total treat.

❹

RESTAURANT PATRICK GUILBAUD
Again, the staff are impeccable. It's almost embarrassing the way they do everything for you, almost to the point of wiping your chin. It reminds me of the sort of place you would get taken out to by your parents, you can almost revert to childhood when you go there.

❺

COOKE'S CAFÉ
Because Johnny Cooke is just great. He does good, reasonable food, always tasty. It makes you want to just hang around.

Leanne de Cerbo is editor of IT magazine

SOUTHSIDE • SANDYMOUNT

SANDYMOUNT

BELLAMY'S FISHERMAN'S WHARF
Mr Bellamy
86 Sandymount Road, Dublin 4
Tel: (01) 660 3802

A fishshop which, unusually, specialises in shellfish – though there is always a good variety of wet fish to be found as well, and lots of useful advice which makes this a valuable address in Sandymount.

● **OPEN:** 8.30am-6.45pm Tue-Sat

BROWNE'S CAFÉ & DELI
Sandymount Green, Sandymount
Dublin 4
Tel: (01) 269 7316

An enduring and well-loved deli, with food to go, and an elegant café. Don't miss their breads.

● **OPEN:** 8am-5.30pm Mon-Fri (deli open to 6pm), 10am-5.30pm Sat, 10.30am-3.30pm Sun

STILLORGAN

CHINA-SICHUAN RESTAURANT ©
David Hui
4 Lower Kilmacud Road, Stillorgan
Tel: (01) 288 4817

David Hui's restaurant easily outpaces its many rivals when it comes to authenticity and the cooking of Chinese food with distinct, vital flavours. They can do certain things - monkfish in yellow bean sauce, or the same fish deep-fried with an excellent sweet and sour sauce; magnificent shredded pork with garlic sauce; thrilling almond bean curd - which are beyond the ability of anyone else, and which can achieve greatness. Add to this some fine vegetable cookery, and a willingness to accede to any particular requests for favourite ways in which to cook a dish, or even to alter their own (they like to mix their tofu with beef, for example) are

SOUTHSIDE ● STILLORGAN

happily acceded to. In addition, the service is excellent, vegetarian creations are excellent, and prices are fair. The room is old fashioned, but the cooking is ageless.

● **OPEN:** 12.30pm-2.30pm Mon-Fri, 1pm-2.30pm Sun, 6pm-11pm Mon-Sun
● **AVERAGE PRICE:** Lunch £8-£10, Dinner £19.50

TERENURE

DOWNEY'S OF TERENURE ©
Mark & John Downey
Terenure Cross, Dublin 6W
Tel: (01) 490 9239

Mark and John Downey, son and father, run a superlative butchers shop, with a large percentage of their meat sourced from organic farmers. To this uncompromising provenance they add some of the best spiced beef you will find, a wonderful range of Ken Moffat's Thornhill ducks and geese, and rarities such as emu, wild boar and ostrich. Father and son have worked tirelessly over the years to expand their range and to source the best meat they can find, and they are amongst the very best in Irish butchery and retailing.

● **OPEN:** 8.30am-6pm Mon-Sat. Delivery service

DANNY O'TOOLE BUTCHERS
Danny O'Toole
138 Terenure Road North, Dublin 6W
Tel: (01) 490 5457

Danny O'Toole's commitment to sourcing and serving organic meat pre-dated all the most recent scares, for some time ago he simply became concerned about animal (and consequently human) welfare, and decided that the mass production of meat was wrong-headed. Subsequent events have, of course, proved him right, and greatly increased his business, which is conducted from this neat shop and from another neat shop in Glasthule. His butchering skills are superlative, which completes the equation of a humanely, environmentally sensitive product brought to his customers in the very optimum way.

● **OPEN:** 9am-6pm Mon-Sat

GREAT DUBLIN RECIPES

Dublin has bequeathed a few celebrated dishes to the cause of good eating, such as its legendary stew of sausages and bacon – Dublin Coddle – and the lavish and rich Dublin Lawyer, a creamy meld of lobster and whiskey.

But as these two recipes, from two of Dublin's most celebrated chefs, **Adrian Roche** of **Jacob's Ladder** and **Derry Clarke** of **L'Ecrivain**, both show, the cooks of the city have always tinkered with the classic dishes of the culinary arts and refashioned them to suit their temperament. Roche and Clarke here improvise on classic ideas, but the results are wholly original and inspiring, and they are two dishes that any visitor or resident needs to have under his or her belt before they can be regarded as true Dubs.

ADRIAN ROCHE'S SHELLFISH CODDLE

Serves 4
12 clams, in their shell
12 cockles, in their shell
12 mussels, in their shell
quarter cup dry white wine
half lb cooked mussel meat, shells removed, juices reserved
12 pieces carrot, blanched
12 pieces of courgette, blanched
12 pieces of potato, cooked
12 pieces of turnip, blanched
quarter cup single cream
2oz chilled butter
12 salmon sausages (see below)
4 oysters, shelled, juices reserved
8 prawns, shelled, raw (optional)
chopped chives

Salmon Sausages:
8oz salmon fillet, dark meat removed
4oz single cream
1 egg white
pinch salt and cayenne pepper
6 large basil leaves, finely shredded

TO MAKE THE SAUSAGE:
Ensure the salmon and cream are well chilled. Place the fish and the egg white and salt in a food processor and puree for about 10 seconds. Using the pulse on your food processor, slowly add the cream until well incorporated. Remove and

sieve. Add the basil leaves and season with the salt and cayenne pepper to taste.

Cut pieces of cling film into 3 inch by 2 inch rectangles. Place a rounded teaspoon of the mixture on each and roll into a sausage shape. Twist and seal. Wrap in tin foil and twist and seal again. Place the sausages in a pot of simmering water and simmer for approximately five minutes. Allow to cool before removing foil and film.

TO ASSEMBLE THE CODDLE:

Heat a deep, heavy-bottomed pan. Place the raw shellfish in their shells, plus the white wine into the pan and steam until just opened. Add the mussels, mussel stock and oyster juice. Bring to the boil. Add the vegetables and cream. While boiling gently, fry the salmon sausages until lightly browned, and warmed through.

Whisk in the chilled butter. Add the sausages, oysters and prawns. Allow to simmer for a few seconds, until the prawns are cooked. Adjust the seasoning and serve sprinkled with the chives.

DERRY CLARKE'S BAKED OYSTERS IN A GUINNESS SABAYON WITH CABBAGE GREENS

Serves 4
The Sabayon:
5 egg yolks
2 tablespoons water
3 tablespoons Guinness
lemon juice to taste
300g (101/2 oz) melted butter

800g (1lb 12oz) Cabbage Greens (use a very leafy cabbage, or substitute spinach) blanched, drained and puréed
4 slices smoked streaky bacon, fried until just crisp and then cut into slivers
24 Oysters (half dozen each), opened, drained

Whisk the eggs, water, Guinness and lemon juice over a warm bain marie until double in size. Whisk in the butter as if you were making mayonnaise (this second whisking can be done in a food processor or with electric beaters).

Mix together the cabbage purée and slivers of bacon and place a spoonful on top of each clean oyster shell. Place an oyster on top. Bake in a hot oven for 1 minute.

Spoon over some sabayon and grill for about five seconds, until golden brown. Serve.

CASTLEKNOCK

BRANGAN & CO
Colm Brangan
15 Deerpark Road
Castleknock
Tel: (01) 821 4052

Colm Brangan's list of wines is sourced only from France, and along with the superstars of Burgundy and Bordeaux, his real speciality lies in discovering great country wines, some of which are absolute corkers and offer great value.

- **OPEN:** Telephone for a list

DEVINE WINE SHOP
Jean Gowing
Main Street
Castleknock
Tel: (01) 820 9027

Jean Gowing runs an excellent and thoughtful wine shop which is helpfully just at the edge of the village of Castleknock. Lots of good advice makes choosing a bottle even more fun.

- **OPEN:** 11am-7pm Mon, 11am-8pm Tue-Sat

LUTTRELLSTOWN CASTLE
Neil McFadden
Castleknock, Dublin 15
Tel: (01) 808 9900

A castle adjoining a serious golf course seems like a strange place to find one of Ireland's most exciting culinary talents, – though don't forget that Robbie Millar works his magic in Shanks, in Northern Ireland, alongside a pair of golf courses. But excitement is exactly what Neil McFadden, who has been here for the last couple of years, can produce on a plate. Sadly, the complex only opens for groups and functions, so individual eaters can't enjoy this fine chef's work at the present time.

- **OPEN:** All year
- **AVERAGE PRICE:** Telephone for group details

CLONTARF

KELLY'S WINE VAULT
Julie Verling
Vernon Avenue, Clontarf
Dublin 3
Tel: (01) 833 5277

Julie Verling is the manager of Kelly's, and with her extensive experience in the trade it bodes well for the company. Also at 25e Malahide Road, Dublin 5.

- **OPEN:** 10.30am-10pm Mon & Sat, 12.30pm-2pm, 4pm-10pm Sun

DRUMCONDRA

IL CORVO
Ali Rashidi
100 Upper Drumcondra Rd
Dublin 9
Tel: (01) 837 5727

A popular little place in Drumcondra, Il Corvo offers familiar food in the Italian style, including very good pizzas, which is just the sort of relaxed cooking every suburb needs.

- **OPEN:** Noon-midnight Mon-Sat, 12.30pm-11pm Sun
- **AVERAGE PRICE:** Meals £15

INDEPENDENT PIZZA CO
Jackie Keating
46 Lower Drumcondra Road
Dublin 9
Tel: (01) 830 2957

The Independent is the classic purveyor of excellent pizzas, the proper composition, cooking and caring of which they take very seriously indeed. A local treasure, for more years than we care to remember.

- **OPEN:** Noon-12.30am Mon-Sat (Fri & Sat till 1am), noon-6.30pm Sun
- **AVERAGE PRICE:** Pizzas £5-£9

DUBLINER'S CHOICE

UNA CARMODY'S FIVE ESSENTIAL ADDRESSES

1

THE MERMAID CAFÉ
for all the good reasons (good staff, great atmosphere) but mostly the food - the macaroni and cauliflower cheese, the tomato risotto, the seafood platter. A greedy person's paradise.

2

THE TROCADERO
Steak, chips and a bottle of red wine. There is no more to be said.

3

THE ELEPHANT AND CASTLE
So obvious that I nearly left it out. Breakfast, dinner and tea.

4

THE MERRION HOTEL
for afternoon tea, which puts all other hotel afternoon teas in the shade.

5

TEMPLE BAR MARKET
Fabulous people and fabulous food.

Una Carmody is Arts Officer for Temple Bar Properties

NORTHSIDE • FAIRVIEW

FAIRVIEW

SWEENEY'S OFF-LICENCE
Finian Sweeney
17 Philipsburg Avenue, Fairview
Dublin 3
Tel: (01) 837 2857
20 Lower Dorset Street, Dublin 1 Tel: (01) 874 9808

Finian Sweeney runs two highly regarded wine shops on the north inner city.

● **OPEN:** 10.30am-10pm Mon-Sat, 12.30pm-2pm, 5pm-10pm Sun

FINGLAS

DUNN'S OF DUBLIN
Peter Dunn
Jamestown Business Park, Finglas
Dublin 11
Tel: (01) 864 3100

Dunn's fine smoked salmon is available in Superquinn stores and specialist outlets, and the wild fish is of a very high standard indeed. They also supply fresh fish and shellfish.

● **OPEN:** Available in Superquinn stores and specialist outlets.

HOWTH

AQUA, AT THE WATER CLUB
Colm Moran
1 West Pier, Howth
Tel: (01) 832 0690 info@aqua.ie

Everyone on the northside is capitalising on sea views, and Aqua is no exception, making the most of the views from the West Pier in Howth. Colm Moran and his team have a stylish restaurant in which to showcase their contemporary cooking, and Aqua is another pleasing sign of the culinary renaissance of north County Dublin.

● **OPEN:** 6.30pm-10pm Mon-Sun, 12.30pm-3pm Thur, Fri & Sun
● **AVERAGE PRICE:** Lunch £14.75, Dinner £25

ORGANIC BOX DELIVERY

The following people and shops organise weekly deliveries of organic foods via the box system.

■ **ABSOLUTELY ORGANIC**
Anne Marie Sheridan
38 Ormond Road, Rathmines, D6   Tel: (01) 4968912

■ **SHEILA BEHAN**
48 Carrick Hill Rise, Portmarnock, Co. Dublin
Tel: (01) 8461276

■ **CAVISTON'S**
59 Glasthule Road, Sandycove, Co. Dublin
Tel: (01) 2809120

■ **COUNTY CELLAR**
Patrick Street, Dun Laoghaire, Co. Dublin
Tel: (01) 2803338

■ **THE GOOD FOOD STORE**
7 Pembroke Lane, Off Baggot Street, D4
Tel: (01) 6675656

■ **DEIRDRE HORGAN**
27 Meadow Close, Rathfarnham, D16
Tel: (01) 2983325

■ **GERRY'S SUPERMARKET**
Main Street, Skerries, Co. Dublin   Tel: (01) 8490404

■ **MAIN ST. FLOWERS**
13 Main Street, Howth, Co. Dublin
Tel: (01) 8395575

■ **GERALDINE KAVANAGH**
25 Darley Street, Harolds Cross, D6
Tel: (01) 4961890

■ **RACHEL MARTIN**
6 St. Kevin's Road, Portobello, D8   Tel: (01) 4536159

■ **CATHERINE NUNES**
35 St. Brignets Villas, Dalkey, Co. Dublin
Tel: (01) 2350123

■ **NATURE STORE**
324A North Circular Road, Phibsboro, D7
Tel: (01) 8304904

■ NOLAN'S SUPERMARKET
49 Vernon Avenue, Clontarf, Dublin 3
Tel: (01) 8336929

■ ORCHARD HEALTHFOODS
Clondalkin, Dublin
Tel: (01) 4570779

■ ORGANIC FOODS LTD
26 Hills Industrial Estate, Lucan, Co. Dublin
Tel: (01) 628 1375

■ DANNY O'TOOLE
Organic Butcher, 138 Terenure Rd Nth, D6
Tel: (01) 4905457

■ TOM O'CONNOR
1B Glasthule Road, Sandycove, Dublin
Tel: (01) 2841125

■ TONY MCGUCKIAN
23 Harmony Avenue, Donnybrook, D4
Tel: (01) 2696634

■ WINKLE NEWSAGENT
3 St.Mobhi Road, Glasnevin, D9 Tel: (01) 8378551

■ GARRISTOWN ORGANIC GROUP
Garristown, Co. Dublin Tel: (01) 8354527

OTHER ESSENTIAL ADDRESSES

■ WHOLEFOODS WHOLESALE
Rosemary Byrne
Unit 2D Kylemore Industrial Estate, Kileen Road,
Dublin 10
Tel: (01) 6262315
Distributor of organic dried goods

■ ORGANIC TRUST LTD
Helen Scully
Vernon House, 2 Vernon Avenue, Clontarf
Tel: (01) 853 0271
This is the administrative home of the Trust, and any enquiries and applications for certification should be directed here.

NORTHSIDE ● HOWTH

CASA PASTA
John Aungier
12 Harbour Road, Howth
Tel: (01) 839 3823
55 Clontarf Road
Dublin 3
Tel: (01) 833 1402

Casa Pasta has been the success story of Howth ever since it opened up in late 1993, spawning a second outpost in recent years in Clontarf and a new branch in Donnybrook. Simple furnishings, keen prices, good views over the bay and straightforward, familiar, zappy food explain the success.

- **OPEN:** Noon-11.30pm Mon-Sun
- **AVERAGE PRICE:** Meals from £10

CITRUS
John Aungier
1 Island View House, Howth
Tel: (01) 832 0200

Under the same ownership as Casa Pasta and just as bustling and boisterous, this is a slick space with magpie modern cooking which pulls in ideas and influences from all over the globe to make very easy-going cooking.

- **OPEN:** 11.30am-11pm Mon-Sun
- **AVERAGE PRICE:** Lunch under £10, Dinner under £20

KING SITRIC
Aidan McManus
East Pier, Howth
Tel: (01) 832 5235

Aidan McManus has bravely redesigned his restaurant, turning it from a clubbable, cosy spot into a bright modern space, and full credit to the man for his ability to reinvent himself after 25 years in the business. His cooking remains rooted in classical French technique, which suits the fish cookery in which the restaurant specialises. Do note that there are also now eight guest rooms where one can stay, all with sea views.

- **OPEN:** 12.30pm-2.30pm, 6pm-10pm Mon-Sat.
- **AVERAGE PRICE:** Lunch over £10, Dinner over £20

NORTHSIDE ● HOWTH

NICKY'S PLAICE
Nicky McLoughlin
Howth Pier, Howth
Tel: (01) 832 3557

This modest little space, right down at the end of the pier in Howth, is still the best place to buy fish amongst the array of shops on the pier. The fish travel only a matter of yards from the boats to the shop, and there is nothing that Nicky doesn't know about filleting and selling them. Delightful.

● **OPEN:** 9am-7.30pm Tue-Wed, 9am-9pm Thu, 9am-6pm Fri, 9am-1pm Sat

MALAHIDE

BON APPETIT
Patsy McGuirk
9 St. James Terrace
Malahide
Tel: (01) 845 0314/845 2206

A clever marriage of the classical and the vernacular repertoire is at the heart of Patsy McGuirk's cooking, and at the heart of Bon Appetit's success. Mr McGuirk cooks in the French style and his food enjoys a comforting familiarity and richness, which is precisely what his customers appreciate.

● **OPEN:** 12.30pm-3pm, 6.30pm-11pm Mon-Sat
● **AVERAGE PRICE:** Lunch over £10, Dinner over £20

CRUZZO
Tom Meenaghan
The Marina, Malahide
Tel: (01) 845 0599

Tom Meenaghan has come over from Conran's huge London restaurant, Mezzo, to head up the team at this smart, ambitious and stonkingly expensive (the developers have allegedly spent £3 million on it) new restaurant. The restaurant is built over the water at the Marina and accessed by a footbridge, so atmospheric views are guaranteed, and Cruzzo wisely serves food which is both classic and achievable, and which has a strong Conranesque accent: confit of duck; spicy chicken wings; calves' liver with red wine sauce and champ;

sea bream with Thai green curry; sole with caper butter; sirloin with onion rings and bearnaise; rich chocolate tart. Given the scale of the restaurant – at 250 seats it is unprecedented in Ireland – this brand new venture will need some time to get all systems running, but the ambition is mightily impressive.

● **OPEN:** 12.30pm-2.30pm Mon-Fri & Sun, 6pm-10.30pm Mon-Sat

SIAM THAI RESTAURANT
Peter Flanagan
Gas Lane, Malahide
Tel: (01) 845 4698

The Siam is a popular restaurant, with accessible, westernised Thai cooking. Main courses are organised under familiar headings - spicy salads, curries, poultry, meat dishes, sweet and sour – to make things easy for entry-level eaters.

● **OPEN:** 6pm-midnight
● **AVERAGE PRICE:** Dinner over £20

MARINO

WRIGHT'S OF MARINO
John Wright
21 Marino Mart, Marino, Dublin 3
Tel: (01) 833 3636

Excellent fish shop with a truly impressive selection.

● **OPEN:** 10am-5pm Tue-Thur, 10am-5.30pm Fri, 10am-2pm Sat

NAUL

THE HERB GARDEN
Denise Dunne
Forde-de-Fyne, Naul, Co Dublin
Tel: (01) 8413907

Denise Dunne produces an outstanding range of herb plants – over 200 varieties – and salad and vegetable plants from her nursery. In addition, she makes a range of oils, mustards and vinegars as well as some chutneys, and sells them in the Saturday Temple Bar market. Denise is also treasurer of Network Organics, a group which covers all aspects of organic production and represents the three certification bodies in Ireland. She also runs a design and landscaping service.

- **OPEN:** Nursery open April-Sept, Sat, Sun, bank holidays 2pm-6pm, other times by appointment

PORTMARNOCK

BISTRO LAMBAY
Helene Corcoran
Unit 4, Strand Road, Portmarnock, Co Dublin
Tel: (01) 846 1120

A popular local seafood place where people return often to eat the same things: spinach crepes, mussels, seafood, pastas and pizzas.

- **OPEN:** 5.30pm-11pm Tue-Sun
- **AVERAGE PRICE:** Dinner £10-£15

JUS DE VINE
Paul Dempsey
Portmarnock Town Centre, Co Dublin
Tel: (01) 846 1192

Paul Dempsey fine wine shop is a vital address in the village.

- **OPEN:** 10.30am-11pm Mon-Sat, 12.30pm-2pm, 4pm-11pm Sun

OSBORNE RESTAURANT
Eric Faussurier
Portmarnock Hotel, Portmarnock, Co Dublin
Tel: (01) 846 0611

Eric Faussurier has been making waves with his cooking in the Portmarnock Hotel, which is affiliated to the local golf course. If that sounds like a bad idea, just consider Robbie Millar's extraordinary success with Shanks in Bangor, and the fact that the talented Neil McFadden is cooking at the Luttrellstown Castle golf complex in Castleknock. Eric is the executive chef and overlooks the Osborne and the more informal Links Brasserie Restaurant.

- **OPEN:** Osborne: 7pm-10.30pm Tue-Sat; Links Brasserie noon-10pm Mon-Sun
- **AVERAGE PRICE:** Osborne dinner: £32.50; Links Brasserie lunch £11-£14, Dinner £17-18

RAHENY

SUPERVALU WINE CENTRE
Colin Shiels
Raheny
Tel: (01) 831 0013

Colin Shiels' fine shop is a great example of just how good and imaginative a supermarket-related wine shop can be.

- **OPEN:** 10.30am-10pm Sun-Thur, 10.30am-10.30pm Fri & Sat

SKERRIES

RED BANK RESTAURANT
Terry McCoy
7 Church Street, Skerries
Tel: (01) 849 1005 Fax: 849 1598
redbank@iol.ie
www.guesthouseireland.com

Terry McCoy's valuable restaurant is an informal, very relaxing place, where the richly enjoyable seafood cookery forms the main attraction. As with most seafood restaurants in Dublin, the style is quite classical and quite rich, and all the better for that, though an old hand like McCoy is not above some modern gestures, and frequently these are very worthwhile. There is lots of character in the cooking: seafood selection Paddy Attley; hake with horseradish - and there are lots of locally sourced foods to complement the main attractions. If you do make it all the way out to Skerries, the Red Bank also offers accommodation. And do try the Red Bank chardonnay – it's splendid.

- **OPEN:** 7pm-10pm Tue-Sat, 12.30pm-3pm Sun
- **AVERAGE PRICE:** Lunch £16, Dinner £25-£27

NORTHSIDE ● CASTLEKNOCK

SMITHFIELD

LITTLE ITALY
Mariese Rabitte
North King Street
Dublin 7
Tel: (01) 872 5208

Little Italy pre-dates our current obsession with artisan Italian foods, offering instead the foods which originally created the image of Italian cooking in these islands: tinned tomatoes; dried pastas; big carafes of rustic wines, cured meats and large-scale production cheeses. For essential store cupboard things such as porcini and risotto rice it is nevertheless an invaluable address.

● **OPEN:** 9am-5pm Mon-Fri, 10am-1pm Sat

KELLY & PING
Sarah Dunne
Chief O'Neills Hotel
Smithfield
Dublin 7
Tel: (01) 817 3840

Having been dormant for decades, Smithfield is being re-built from the ground up at a ferocious speed, and the opening of smart new ventures like Kelly & Ping bodes well for the area. They serve simple fusion food, mainly Asiatic things such as coconuty curries and nasi goreng and other Eastern classics, served in white bowls with rice or noodles served separately. They have a fine range of Asian beers also.

● **OPEN:** Noon-11pm Mon-Sun (from 6pm Sat, all day buffet Sun)

PADDY'S PLACE
Paddy Donnelly
Corporation Markets
Smithfield
Tel (01) 873 5130

A little caff in the middle of the Corporation markets, where you can find Dublin coddle, beef stew, and fresh fish.

● **OPEN:** 6am-2.30pm Mon-Fri, 7am-11am Sat

NORTHSIDE ● STONEYBATTER

STONEYBATTER
TA SE MAHAGONI GASPIPES
Drina Kinsley
17 Manor Street
Stoneybatter
Tel: (01) 679 8138

Enjoyable American-style cooking from Drina Kinsley and a late night jazz menu and music is the formula of this enduring northside restaurant, on the main strip of Stoneybatter.

- **OPEN:** 1pm-4pm Tue-Fri, 7pm-midnight Tue-Thur, 7pm-2am Fri-Sat
- **AVERAGE PRICE:** Lunch under £10, Dinner over £15

SWORDS
THE CHUCK WAGON
Martin Crosby
The N1, just north of Swords dual-carriageway

Some days, it is almost difficult to make out the tiny cabin which is the Chuck Wagon, so deep and dense is the throng of hungry truckers besieging this beloved little caff.
A lot of truckers – and ourselves – order the sausage and bacon soda bread sarnie with onions with such frequency that you would imagine there was nothing else on the menu. There are lots of other things, but the bacon and soda gets our vote as the best on-the-road food in the country.

- **OPEN:** 8am-7pm Mon-Sat

LORD MAYOR'S OFF LICENCE
Larry Cullen
Swords
Co Dublin
Tel: (01) 840 9662

You will find a great selection of wines and spirits in this smart, if dimly-lit, shop.

- **OPEN:** 10.30am-10.30pm Mon-Sun (till 10pm Sun)

NORTHSIDE ● SWORDS

LUKAS
Kate Gibbons
River Mall, Main Street, Swords
Tel: (01) 840 9080

This little restaurant is on the first floor of the mall, and is a popular local place for home made pastas, as well as quesadillas and other Tex-Mex dishes cooked by head chef Denis Murnane.

- **OPEN:** Dinner Mon-Sat
- **AVERAGE PRICE:** Dinner £16

THE OLD SCHOOLHOUSE
Paul Lewis
Coolbanagher, Swords,
Co Dublin
Tel: (01) 840 2846

The Old Schoolhouse is a capable, comfortable restaurant, sharply tuned into the demands of its suburban clientele. Paul Lewis has been in the kitchens for some years now, and his confidence and experience is evident.

- **OPEN:** 12.30pm-2.30pm Mon-Fri, 6.30pm-11.30pm Mon-Sat
- **AVERAGE PRICE:** Lunch £10, Dinner £20

SANBOS
Gail Sinclair
Plaza Mall, Swords
Co Dublin
Tel: (01) 840 8668

Sanbos is the new kid on the block in Swords, "and I am keen to introduce Swords to food like panini, goats' cheese, black olive paste and real coffee," says Gail Sinclair, whom many will recall from her days running Malahide's much-missed Old Street Wine Bar.
Sandwiches can be assembled from pretty much whatever takes your fancy, and there are 8 different types of coffee as well as teas and chocolates. Deliveries can also be arranged within the area, so long as one telephones in advance.

- **OPEN:** 8am–5pm, Mon–Sat

WHERE TO STAY

The huge number of new hotels which have opened in Dublin in recent years shows little sign of slowing down, with both a Hilton Hotel and a Four Seasons Hotel due to open soon, as we write. How they will fare will be interesting to watch, not just because there is now over-capacity in Dublin, but because Dubliners traditionally don't take to hotel and restaurant chains.

The following are some favourite places to stay.

BOUTIQUE HOTELS

THE CLARENCE
6-8 Wellington Quay, D2
Tel: (01) 670 9000 clarence@indigo.ie

Dublin's first boutique hotel boasts one of the capital's great restaurants – The Tea Rooms – and a design style which is soulfully gorgeous and enticing – big Guggi paintings (yeah, we also knew him before he was an art world superstar), Lutyens chairs; definitive West Cork furniture, a superb mix of design features which makes it sublimely relaxing. The service should be sharper than it is, and for the high prices they charge it really should always be on the money, which is sometimes not the case, but if you can afford it, then The Clarence is someplace special. Breakfasts are particularly good. B&B from £195

THE MORGAN ©
10 Fleet Street, D2
Tel: (01) 679 3939 Fax: 679 3946
sales@themorgan.com www.themorgan.com

The curious thing about the Morgan is that it manages to feel like such a superb hideaway, even though it is right smack on Fleet Street, a stone's throw from Westmoreland Street and Temple Bar. Moodily minimalist, it is also fiercely disciplined and successful – these are amongst the most successful rooms in the city, all of them personalised and svelte. Breakfast is served in the bedrooms, as there is no dining room, which adds to the away-from-it-all ambience. Unfortunately, the good taste ran out before they got around to doing the downstairs bar and the All Sports Café, both of which should be rethought soonest. B&B from £105

THE MORRISON
Ormond Quay, Dublin 1 Tel: (01) 878 2999

Many folk find the John Rocha-designed Morrison to be too gloomy in design, its Asiatic browns and blacks and dark

WHERE TO STAY

wood too moody to really create a feeling of wellbeing. Whilst the Halo restaurant is very successful, and Jean-Michel Poulot shows some terrifically impressive and accomplished fusion cooking, the public bars are less good, but we have to confess to finding the bedrooms very assured and complete and comfortable, with the interplay between black and white very well realised. Anthony Kenna manages the hotel with considerable grace, and a front bedroom with view of the Liffey is a treat, albeit a pricey one. Their new sushi bar, Lobo, is just open. B&B £155 per room

OTHER HOTELS

BEWLEY'S HOTEL AT NEWLAND'S CROSS
Newlands Cross, Naas Rd, Dublin
Tel: (01) 464 0140 Fax: 464 0900
res@bewleys.com bewleyshotels.com
The location is extra-convenient if you need to use the airport or the ferries, or if getting away from the city is a priority. But, aside from a handy location, what the Bewley's Hotel offers is the best value you can find: a £49 flat rate for rooms which are spacious and well finished, and simply perfect for families. A second branch, the Bewley's Aparthotel in Ballsbridge, also offers good value (£69 per room) but the rooms are much less comfortable and successful than at Newland's Cross. Rooms at £49.

FITZWILLIAM PARK HOTEL
No. 5 Fitzwilliam Square
Tel: (01) 662 8280 info@fitzpark.ie www.fitzpark.ie
A front room on the fourth floor of the lovely Fitzwilliam Park offers a true treat: wake up in the morning, pull back the curtains, and you look out over the city's most glorious Georgian square and out over the rooftops of the city. It's glorious. The view is less edifying in the evenings, however, when poor unfortunate women use the square to ply their trade. Catherine O'Reilly runs a good, small, specialist hotel with magnificent skill, and the understated nature of the Fitzwilliam is a treat. Breakfasts are good, the location superb. B&B from £70

THE HIBERNIAN
Eastmoreland Place, Ballsbridge, Dublin 4
Tel: (01) 668 7666 info@hibernianhotel.ie
Fantastic staff make all the difference in David Butt's excellent hotel, located in a nicely quiet part of Ballsbridge, yet only a few minutes' walk from the centre of town. B&B from £120

WHERE TO STAY

THE MERRION HOTEL
Merrion Street, Dublin 2
Tel: (01) 603 0600 info@merrionhotel.ie
Sumptuous and expensive, the Merrion Hotel houses both Restaurant Patrick Guilbaud and its own Mornington's Restaurant where Ed Cooney cooks. Its location is superb, of course, and the restoration of the hotel has been achieved with terrific skill. The Merrion's public rooms have become a very popular spot for taking a serious afternoon tea in the old style: lots of delicate sandwiches, and tiered cake stands. Expensive, of course, but a rather nice antidote to the overheated workings of the city. B&B from £150.

RADISSON SAS ST. HELEN'S HOTEL
Stillorgan Road, Blackrock Tel: (01) 218 6000
Ailish Carew's staff understand the meaning of service, and their politeness and helpfulness creates the successful atmosphere of the Radisson and explains its success. The rooms are not great, and even the suites can seem a little cramped, but the amiability of the Talavera Restaurant in the basement is very winning. There has been a recent change of chef in the more formal Le Panto restaurant. Bar lunches are good and extremely popular. B&B from £150

GUEST HOUSES

ANGLESEA HOUSE
63 Anglesea Road, Ballsbridge, D4 Tel: (01) 668 3877
Helen Kirrane's lovely guesthouse serves what is not just the finest breakfast in the city, but what may well be the finest breakfast in the country. Course after course of delicious things flow from the kitchen, and one time breakfast here concluded with some chocolate profiteroles – we're not making this up. There is no treat quite like it. B&B from £45

BUTLERS TOWN HOUSE
44 Lansdowne Road, Ballsbridge, D4 Tel: (01) 667 4022
Chris Voss runs a good house, literally a stone's throw from the Lansdowne Road stadium (in fact, match officials stay here when international matches are being played). The rooms are comfortable, individual and airy, breakfasts are good. B&B from £45

NUMBER 31 Ⓒ
31 Leeson Close, D2
Tel: (01) 676 5011 number31@iol.ie
This cult address mixes a modernist townhouse which is quite gorgeous with a Georgian house which is very tradi-

WHERE TO STAY

tional, and which offers some of the largest rooms in the city. Noel and Deirdre Comer are superb hosts, and do remember to save a "Good morning!" for Homer, the dog. B&B from £42 pps.

WATERLOO HOUSE
Waterloo Road, Dublin 4 Tel: (01) 660 1888
waterloohouse@eircom.net
Evelyn Corcoran runs an excellent and very comfortable house, and what people love is the chance to stay in a Georgian house in such a pleasant and quiet location. B&B from £42.50

SELF-CATERING SUITES, RENTAL HOUSES

LATCHFORD'S APARTMENTS
99/100 Lower Baggot Street, D2 Tel: (01) 676 0784
The apartments here are above Frank Latchford's eponymous bistro, and offer good value for money for such a central location. They range between studios and superior studios, 1 and 2-bedroomed apartments. Car parking is available for a small sum. £79-£99 per night

MOLESWORTH COURT
Schoolhouse Lane, D2 Tel: (01) 676 4799
Accommodation ranges from a one bedroom unit to a three bedroom penthouse suite. Good value, given the location, and the decoration is stylish. £95-£200 per night

STEPHEN'S HALL HOTEL
Earlsfort Centre, Lwr Leeson St, D2
Tel: (01) 661 0585
The Stephen's Hall hotel is an all-suite hotel, and the rooms are spacious. The company also operate the Premier Portfolio, which offers over 50 fully serviced apartments in Dublin 2 and 4. There is car parking. £85-£170

BUDGET ACCOMMODATION

JURY'S CHRISTCHURCH INN
Christchurch Place, D8 Tel: (01) 454 0000
Jury's Custom House Inn, Custom House Quay, D1
Tel: (01) 607 5000
The Jury's Inns are both well located close to the centre of the city, and their set room rate means they are good value for families.

OUT OF TOWN

RESTAURANTS

AVOCA HANDWEAVRS
Kilmacanogue, Co Wicklow
Tel: (01) 286 7466
Powerscourt House, Enniskerry
Tel: (01) 204 6070
There is nothing nicer than a trip southside to these two celebrated lunchtime restaurants, at Powerscourt and Kilmacanogue. Superb food, cool shops, fantastic atmosphere. Lunch on the terrace at Powerscourt is a treat.

THE TREE OF IDLENESS
Bray, Co Wicklow
Tel: (01) 286 3498
Fantastic Greek-Cypriot cooking from young Robert Fitzharris in Susan Courtellas' unique restaurant.

WEEKENDS AWAY

BECKETT'S
Leixlip, Co Kildare
Tel: (01) 624 7040
A new venture, by John O'Byrne of Dublin's legendary Dobbins restaurant, is housed in a Cooldrinagh House and offers accommodation along with a restaurant for Ireland's silicon valley IT set.

THE BROOK LODGE INN
Macreddin Village, Co Wicklow
Tel: (0402) 36444 brooklodge@macreddin.ie
Evan Doyle located his country hotel and restaurant so that one could be here in an hour from Donnybrook church. Still early days, but Doyle's management and Freda Wolfe's cooking in The Strawberry Tree should create a fine address.

GHAN HOUSE
Carlingford, Co Louth
Tel: (042) 9373682 ghanhouse@eircom.net
Handsome house at the edge of Carlingford, with a good restaurant.

HANORA'S COTTAGE
Nire Valley, Co Waterford
Tel: (052) 36134
Extraordinary breakfasts, the stunning beauty of the Nire Valley to walk in and Eoin Wall's good cooking.

OUT OF TOWN

HILTON PARK
Clones, Co Monaghan
Tel: (047) 56007 jm@hiltonpark.ie
A gorgeous, grand house and fine cooking. Weekend rates.

JORDAN'S TOWNHOUSE
Carlingford, Co Louth
Tel: (042) 9373223 jordons@iol.ie
A Carlingford classic, with comfortable rooms and excellent cooking from Harry and Marian Jordan.

KILGRANEY HOUSE
Bagenalstown, Co Carlow
Tel: (0503) 75283
A gorgeous house, and a cult weekend address with super cooking.

THE LORD BAGENAL INN
Leighlinbridge, Co Carlow
Tel: (0503) 21668 info@lordbagenal.com
The rooms are very comfortable at James Kehoe's canal-side bar and restaurant. Splendid art collection.

SALVILLE HOUSE
Enniscorthy, Co Wexford
Tel: 054) 35252 salvillehouse@eircom.net
Gorgeous, simple house with inspiring cooking from Gordon Parker.

TEMPLE COUNTRY HOUSE & SPA
Horseleap, Co Westmeath
Tel: (0506) 35118 templespa@spiders.ie
Believe us, you just won't want to leave to head back to the big smoke.

TINAKILLY HOUSE
Rathnew, Co Wicklow
Tel: (0404) 69274 reservations @tinakilly.ie
Josephine and Raymond Power have taken over from their parents at this fine address, nicely proximate to the capital. Personable staff and good cooking create a very relaxing address.

TONLEGEE HOUSE
Athy, Co Kildare
Tel: (0507) 31473 tonlegehouse@eircom.net
Marjorie Molloy runs a lovely house and restaurant, just outside Athy.

INDEX

Absolutely Organic **108**
Africana Restaurant **47**
Al Minar **76**
Al Tayibat **47**
Angelo, Cafe **87**
Anglesea House **120**
Anne Rossiter Foods **28**
Aprile, C **87**
Aqua, at The Water Club **107**
Ar Vicoletto **60**
Aroma Bistro & Paninis **50**
Arthouse **59**
Asia Market **12**
Asian Food Store **47**
Auriga, Cafe **19**
Avoca Handweavers **122**
AYA **12**
Ayumi-Ya **70**
Baccaro, Il **12**
Bad Ass Café **13**
Bailey, The **63**
Ballsbridge **66**
Ballycomber Meats **89**
Bang Café **13**
Bangkok Café **14**
Batts **66**
Beckett's **122**
Belgo **14**
Bella Cuba **66**
Bellamy's Fisherman's Wharf **100**
Benny's Fish & Chips **87**
Bernardos **14**
Berry Bros & Rudd **15**
Beshoff Brother's **87**
Best of Italy **91**
Bewley's Hotel at Newland's Cross **119**
Bewley's Oriental Café **15**
Big Cheese Company **15, 50**
Bijou Bistro **95**
Bistro Lambay **113**
Bistro One **86**
Blackrock **70**
Blazing Salads II **16**
Blueberry's **71**
Bloomfields **89**
Bombay Pantry **82**
Bon Appetit **111**
Borza's **87**
Botticelli **16**
Brangan & Co **104**
Brasserie Na Mara **82**
Brazen Head **63**
Bretzel Kosher Bakery **90**
Brewbaker's **74**
Brook Lodge Inn **99, 122**
Brown's Bar **74**
Browne's Brasserie **16**
Browne's Café & Deli **100**
Bruno's **17**
Bu-Ali **17**
Burdock's, Leo **19**
Burgundy Direct **71**
Butler's Chocolate Café **74**
Butler's Pantry **71**
Butlers Town House **120**
Cabinteely **76**
Cafe Angelo **87**
Café Auriga **19**
Café En Seine **65**
Café Inn **74**
Café Irie **74**
Café Java **74**
Café Mao **40**
Café Ole **46**
Caffe Fresca **50**
Caffola's **87**
Cakes & Co **72**
Carmines **96**
Casa Pasta **110**
Castleknock **104**
Catherine Nunes **108**
Cave, La **19**
Caviston's **83, 108**
Caviston's Seafood Bar **50**
Cedar Tree **20**
Chameleon, The **20**
Chapter One **22**
Chez Emily **26**
Chili Club **22**
China-Sichuan Restaurant **100**
Chocolate Bar, The **65**

INDEX

Choice's Afro World Boutique 47
Chompy's 74
Chuck Wagon 116
Citrus 110
Clarence, The 118
Clontarf 105
Coffee Club 74
Commons Restaurant 22
Cooke's Café 23
Coq Hardi, Le 66
Corleggy Cheese 26
Cornucopia 23
Corte, La 50
Corvo, Il 105
County Cellar 108
Crema 96
Creme de la Creme 50
Cruzzo 111
Da Pino 23
Dail Bia 24
Dali's 72
Dalkey 76
Daniel Finnegan 77
Danny O'Toole 101, 109
Davy Byrne's 63
Deirdre Horgan 108
Deveney's Off Licence 97
DeVine Wine Shop 104
Diep Le Shaker 24
Dish 24
Dobbins Wine Bar 25
Docker's, The 63
Doheny & Nesbitt's 63
Don Giovannis 77
Donnybrook 79
Douglas Food Co 79
Downey's of Terenure 101
Druid Chocolates 25
Drumcondra 105
Drumeel Farm 26
Dublin Brewing Company 63
Dublin Food Co-Op 29
Duke, The 63
Dun Laoghaire 82
Dunn's of Dublin 107
Dunne & Crescenzi 26, 29
Dunnes Stores 18
Dunville Place 92
Eden 30
Elephant & Castle 31
Ely 31
Epicurean Food Mall 50
Erlich's Kosher Butcher 47
Ernies 80
Expresso Bar 67
Fairview 107
Fallon's 63
Findlater 32
Finglas 107
Fitzers Cafés 67
Fitzwilliam Park Hotel 119
Forde de Fynde Herbs 26
Fothergill's 97
Fox's Famous Seafood Kitchen 64
Foxrock 86
Freres Jacques, Les 32
Front Lounge, The 65
Furama Chinese Restaurant 80
Fusciardi's 87
Gallic Kitchen 27, 33
Gammells 92
Garristown Organic Group 109
Gerry's Supermarket 108
Ghan House 122
Glann Gourmet Sauces 27
Glencarn Foods 27
Globe, The 65
Gloria Jean's Coffee Co 74
Goatstown 86
Good Food Store 68, 108
Good World Restaurant 33
Gotham Café 33
Gourmet France 67
Gourmet Gallery 97
Gourmet Store 95
Grogan's Castle Lounge 64
Guilbaud, Restaurant Patrick 34
Guy Stuart 34
Hacket, CP 89

INDEX

Halo **35**
Hanora's Cottage **122**
Harbourmaster, The **34**
Harvey's Coffee House **74**
Healys Vegetables & Fruit **27**
Hemingways of Ballsbridge **68**
Herb Garden, The **112**
Hibernian Hotel **68, 119**
Hick's Butchers **27, 85**
Hilton Park **122**
Hogan's **65**
Horseshoe Bar **64**
Howth **107**
Il Baccaro **12**
Il Corvo **105**
Il Primo **49**
Imperial Chinese Restaurant **35**
Independent Pizza Co **105**
Insomnia Coffee Company **74**
International Bar **64**
Islamic Centre **47**
Islamic Cultural Centre **47**
Istanbul **50**
Itsabagel **51**
Jacob's Ladder **35, 102**
Joose Bar **36**
Jordan's Townhouse **123**
Joy of Coffee **74**
Juice **36**
Jury's Christchurch Inn **121**
Jus de Vine **113**
Kaffe Moka **51**
Kavanagh's **64**
Kavanagh, Geraldine **108**
Keegan's of Ranelagh **92**
Kehoe's **64**
Kelly & Ping **115**
Kelly's Wine Vault **105**
Kenny's **64**
Khyber Tandoori **36**
Kiernan's, Damien, Supervalu **18**
Kilgraney House **123**
Kilkenny Design **37**
King Sitric **110**
Kitchen Complements **37**
L'Ecrivain **29, 103**
La Cave **19**
La Corte **50**
La Stampa **55**
La Tavola **73**
Latchford's Apartments **121**
Le Coq Hardi **66**
Leo Burdock's **19**
Les Freres Jacques **32**
Leyden's Fine Wines **51**
Life Café-Bar **65**
Little Caesar's Palace **38**
Little Italy **115**
Lobo **99**
Lobster Pot Restaurant **69**
Locks **90**
Long Hall, The **64**
Lord Bagenal Inn **123**
Lord Edward Seafood Restaurant **38**
Lord Mayor's Off Licence **116**
Lukas **117**
Luttrellstown Castle **104**
Magills **38**
Mahagoni Gaspipes, Ta Se **116**
Main St. Flowers **108**
Maison de Gourmet **39**
Malahide **111**
Mange Tout **39**
Mao, Café **40**
Marino **112**
Martin, Rachel **108**
McCabe's Wine Merchants **72**
McDaid's **64**
McGuckian, Tony **109**
Mermaid Café **40**
Merrion Hotel **120**
Messrs Maguire **63**
Metro, The **59**
Milano **41**
Mitchell's **41**

INDEX

Molesworth Court **121**
Molloy's of Donnybrook **81**
Monkstown **88**
Morel's Bistro **85**
Morels at Stephen's Hall **42**
Morgan, The **118**
Morrison, The **118**
Morton's **18, 98**
Mulligan's **64**
Mulloy, Thomas **42**
Munkberry's **77**
Muscat **42**
National Museum Café **43**
Natural Food Partnership **51**
Nature Store **108**
Naul **112**
Neary's **64**
Nectar Juice Bar **92**
Nicky's Plaice **111**
Nico's **43**
Nolan's Supermarket **108**
Norseman, The **65**
Nude **43**
Number 31 **120**
Number Ten Restaurant **44**
O'Briens Fine Wines **81**
O'Connell's **69**
O'Connor, Tom **109**
O'Donoghue's **64**
O'Toole's Butchers **85**
O'Toole, Danny **109, 101**
Octagon Bar **65**
Oddbins **44**
Odeon Bar Restaurant **45, 65**
Old Dublin **45**
Old Mill **46**
Old Schoolhouse **117**
Olive Tree, The (Blackrock) **72**
Olive Tree, The (Goatstown) **86**
Olvi Oils **28**
On The Grapevine **77**
101 Talbot **46**
One Pico **46**
Orchard Healthfoods **109**
Organic Box Delivery **108**
Organic Foods Ltd **109**
Organic Shop, The **51**
Organic Trust Ltd **109**
Osborne Restaurant **113**
Pad Thai **90**
Paddy's Place **115**
Palace, The **64**
Panem **48**
Pasta Fresca **48**
PD's Woodhouse **79**
Peacock Alley **48**
Petit des Gourmets, Le **51**
Pino, Da **23**
Poppadom **95**
Porterhouse, The **63**
Portmarnock **113**
Portobello **90**
Pravda **65**
Primo, Il **49**
Pronto **93**
Punjab Balti House **93**
Purty Kitchen **88**
Queen of Tarts **74**
Queen's, The **78**
QV2 **49**
Radisson SAS St. Helen's Hotel **120**
Ragazzi **78**
Raheny **114**
Rajdoot Tandoori **52**
Ranelagh **91**
Rathgar **95**
Rathmines **96**
Rathsallagh House **123**
Read, Thomas **65**
Real Olive Co **28**
Recipes **102**
Red Bank Restaurant **114**
Redmonds **93**
Restaurant Patrick Guilbaud **34**
Rhino Room **23**
Ristorante Da Roberta **72**
Roches Stores **18**

INDEX

Rodney's Bistro 76
Roly's Bistro 70
Rossini's 78
Roy Fox 80
Rubicon 52
Runner Bean 52
Ryan's 64
Saagar 52
Sabores de Mexico 28
Salville House 123
Sanbos 117
Sandra's Choice 51
Sandymount 100
Searsons 88
Senor Sassi's 53
Shalimar, The 53
Sheehan's 64
Sheila Behan 108
Sheridan's Cheesemongers 28, 54
Siam Thai Restaurant 112
Simon's Place 54
Sinners 54
Skerries 114
Slattery's 64
Smithfield 115
Spice of Life 51
St Helen's Hotel 120
St. Martin Shellfish 28
Stag's Head 55, 64
Stephen's Hall Hotel 121
Steps of Rome 55
Stillorgan 100
Stoneybatter 116
Superquinn 18
Supervalu 18
Supervalu Wine Centre 114
Supper's Ready 56
Sweeney O'Rourke 56
Sweeney's Off-Licence 107
Swords 116
Ta Se Mahagoni Gaspipes 116
Tea Rooms 56
Teko & Sons 47
Temple Bar Market 26
Temple Bar, The 65
Temple Country House & Spa 123
Terenure 101
Terroirs 81
Tesco's 18
Thai House 79
Thomas Mulloy 42
Thomas Read 65
Thomas' Delicatessen 86
Thornton's 91
Tinakilly House 123
Toner's 64
Tonlegee House 123
Tosca 57
Trastevere 57
Tree of Idleness 122
Trocadero 57
Tropical Shop 47
Tropical Stop Centre 47
Tulsi 58
Turk's Head 65
Unicorn Restaurant 58
Valentia Cookery 76
Valparaiso 88
Vaughan Johnson 58
Velure Bar & Restaurant 60
Vico, The 78
Vintry, The 96
Wabbit Co, The 28
Wagamama 60
Waterloo House 121
West Coast Coffee Company 74
Wholefoods Wholesale 109
Winding Stair Bookshop & Cafe 61, 74
Winkle Newsagent 109
Wright's of Marino 112
Yamamori Noodles 61
Zafraan 61
Zanzibar 65
Zen Chinese Restaurant 98